BORDER SECURITY GADGETS, GIZMOS, AND INFORMATION: USING TECHNOLOGY TO INCREASE SITUATIONAL AWARENESS AND OPERATIONAL CONTROL

HEARING

BEFORE THE

SUBCOMMITTEE ON BORDER AND MARITIME SECURITY

OF THE

COMMITTEE ON HOMELAND SECURITY HOUSE OF REPRESENTATIVES

ONE HUNDRED FOURTEENTH CONGRESS

SECOND SESSION

MAY 24, 2016

Serial No. 114–72

Printed for the use of the Committee on Homeland Security

Available via the World Wide Web: http://www.gpo.gov/fdsys/

U.S. GOVERNMENT PUBLISHING OFFICE

23–244 PDF WASHINGTON : 2017

For sale by the Superintendent of Documents, U.S. Government Publishing Office
Internet: bookstore.gpo.gov Phone: toll free (866) 512–1800; DC area (202) 512–1800
Fax: (202) 512–2104 Mail: Stop IDCC, Washington, DC 20402–0001

COMMITTEE ON HOMELAND SECURITY

MICHAEL T. MCCAUL, Texas, *Chairman*

LAMAR SMITH, Texas
PETER T. KING, New York
MIKE ROGERS, Alabama
CANDICE S. MILLER, Michigan, *Vice Chair*
JEFF DUNCAN, South Carolina
TOM MARINO, Pennsylvania
LOU BARLETTA, Pennsylvania
SCOTT PERRY, Pennsylvania
CURT CLAWSON, Florida
JOHN KATKO, New York
WILL HURD, Texas
EARL L. "BUDDY" CARTER, Georgia
MARK WALKER, North Carolina
BARRY LOUDERMILK, Georgia
MARTHA MCSALLY, Arizona
JOHN RATCLIFFE, Texas
DANIEL M. DONOVAN, JR., New York

BENNIE G. THOMPSON, Mississippi
LORETTA SANCHEZ, California
SHEILA JACKSON LEE, Texas
JAMES R. LANGEVIN, Rhode Island
BRIAN HIGGINS, New York
CEDRIC L. RICHMOND, Louisiana
WILLIAM R. KEATING, Massachusetts
DONALD M. PAYNE, JR., New Jersey
FILEMON VELA, Texas
BONNIE WATSON COLEMAN, New Jersey
KATHLEEN M. RICE, New York
NORMA J. TORRES, California

BRENDAN P. SHIELDS, *Staff Director*
JOAN V. O'HARA, *General Counsel*
MICHAEL S. TWINCHEK, *Chief Clerk*
I. LANIER AVANT, *Minority Staff Director*

SUBCOMMITTEE ON BORDER AND MARITIME SECURITY

MARTHA MCSALLY, ARIZONA, *Chairman*

LAMAR SMITH, Texas
MIKE ROGERS, Alabama
CANDICE S. MILLER, Michigan
JEFF DUNCAN, South Carolina
LOU BARLETTA, Pennsylvania
WILL HURD, Texas
MICHAEL T. MCCAUL, Texas *(ex officio)*

FILEMON VELA, Texas
LORETTA SANCHEZ, California
SHEILA JACKSON LEE, Texas
BRIAN HIGGINS, New York
NORMA J. TORRES, California
BENNIE G. THOMPSON, Mississippi *(ex officio)*

PAUL L. ANSTINE, *Subcommittee Staff Director*
KRIS CARLSON, *Subcommittee Clerk*
ALISON NORTHROP, *Minority Subcommittee Staff Director*

CONTENTS

Page

STATEMENTS

The Honorable Martha McSally, a Representative in Congress From the State of Arizona, and Chairwoman, Subcommittee on Border and Maritime Security:
Oral Statement 1
Prepared Statement 3
The Honorable Filemon Vela, a Representative in Congress From the State of Texas, and Ranking Member, Subcommittee on Border and Maritime Security 4
The Honorable Bennie G. Thompson, a Representative in Congress From the State of Mississippi, and Ranking Member, Committee on Homeland Security:
Prepared Statement 5

WITNESSES

Mr. Ronald Vitiello, Acting Chief, U.S. Border Patrol, U.S. Department of Homeland Security:
Oral Statement 7
Joint Prepared Statement 11
Mr. Major General Randolph D. "Tex" Alles, (Ret.–USMC), Executive Assistant Commissioner, Office of Air and Marine Operations, U.S. Customs and Border Protection, U.S. Department of Homeland Security:
Oral Statement 8
Joint Prepared Statement 11
Mr. Mark Borkowski, Assistant Commissioner and Chief Acquisition Executive, Office of Technology Innovation and Acquisition, U.S. Customs and Border Protection, U.S. Department of Homeland Security:
Oral Statement 9
Joint Prepared Statement 11
Ms. Rebecca Gambler, Director, Homeland Security and Justice, U.S. Government Accountability Office:
Oral Statement 17
Prepared Statement 18

BORDER SECURITY GADGETS, GIZMOS, AND INFORMATION: USING TECHNOLOGY TO INCREASE SITUATIONAL AWARENESS AND OPERATIONAL CONTROL

Tuesday, May 24, 2016

U.S. House of Representatives,
Committee on Homeland Security,
Subcommittee on Border and Maritime Security,
Washington, DC.

The subcommittee met, pursuant to call, at 2:53 p.m., in Room 311, Cannon House Office Building, Hon. Martha McSally [Chairwoman of the subcommittee] presiding.

Present: Representatives McSally, Rogers, Duncan, Hurd, Vela, Torres, and Thompson (ex officio).

Ms. McSally. The Committee on Homeland Security, Subcommittee on Border and Maritime Security will come to order. The subcommittee is meeting today to examine CBP's procurement and use of technology to secure the Southern Border. I recognize myself for an opening statement.

First, let me say thanks for your patience. I know we are now nearly an hour behind. We will try to be as expeditious as possible. We value your time, but you never know when votes are going to come up. So I appreciate your grace and your patience with that.

The Southwest Border of the United States is home to nearly 2,000 miles of majestic, yet rugged and often treacherous terrain, terrain that makes Border Patrol access in some remote areas a mere impossible proposition. Manpower alone, while essential, will never be enough to secure the border. In order to enhance situational awareness, we need to leverage technological force multipliers that provide persistent surveillance across wide swaths of remote areas along the border.

Technology such as cameras, night vision goggles, motion sensors, and surveillance equipment have become critical elements of our border security operations. These technologies have enhanced agent safety, provide a constant monitoring of difficult-to-access areas, and extended situational awareness, and the ability to interdict criminal activity faster.

Aviation assets, such unmanned aerial vehicles, or UAVs, often considered UASs, unmanned aerial systems, equipped with advanced radar capabilities, have also refined our understanding of the significant threat that exists along the border, and help reposition and redeploy assets as the flow and the vulnerability shift. But technology cannot do any of these things if CBP's acquisition and procurement process cannot get these tools and the latest cutting-edge technology in the hands of the men and women on the ground in a timely fashion.

Situation awareness is contingent on feeding information from centralized operation centers far from the border down to the individual agent level, so they can actually respond accordingly. Technology has to be focused on meeting the immediate needs of the agent, and not stovepiped into a command center. I speak to this from first-hand information. I have more experience than I would prefer to have in some cases on, you know, time-sensitive targeting, on operations centers in the military, and so these challenges are similar as far as merging together information providing a good common operational picture, situation awareness, but not just to the generals, but to the troops and those that are actually doing the mission. So that is always going to be my sort-of frame of mind. Although it is not the same as in the military, there are similar challenges as far as using technology, fusing information, and providing real-time, near-time decision quality information to leadership and to those that are out there on the front lines.

CBP's border technology procurement efforts, to put it mildly, have a bit of a checkered history of not delivering timely acquisitions that include more failures than successes, including the Secure Border Initiative, coastal interceptor vessel, ultralight aircraft detection, and mobile surveillance capability, which have all become synonymous with a deeply troubled acquisition process. These procurements have run over budget, behind schedule, been subject to litigation, and wasted a good deal of taxpayer dollars to boot. In this time of limited budgets, we cannot afford to waste $1 billion on a failed system to learn what not to do. Border security cannot continue to be held back by a system that has an astonishing lack of urgency in getting it done for the people on the ground.

Our agents and officers in the field desperately need the capability they have asked for to do the job. But on the whole, I don't believe CBP's Office of Technology Innovation and Acquisition, OTIA, has delivered. OTIA's mission is to identify and acquire products and services to improve CBP's performance in securing the borders.

OTIA has been the lead agency responsible for acquiring technologies associated with the Arizona technology plant. As far as I can tell, the only procurement that is working well and is on budget is the integrated fixed tower program located principally in my district. However, this comes after chronic delays and the cancellation of SBInet. Now on track, Chief Vitiello recently certified to Congress that the program meets its operational requirements.

With the exception of that outlier, industry officials we have spoken to tell us over and over again, CBP's requirements are often poorly drafted, ill-defined, and, perhaps, most alarmingly not stable. Transparency is also a challenge as the CBP's ability to forecast their needs so industry can spend the research and development dollars to mature technology for use in border security applications.

The Government Accountability Office, GAO, has, on several occasions, criticized CBP for not following aspects of DHS's acquisition management guidance with the Arizona border technology plant and the lack of performance metrics to determine if the cost is worth the border security improvement.

As a result of CBP's troubling procurement record, I authored the Border Security Technology Accountability Act that ensures border security programs are meeting costs, schedule, and performance thresholds, and that technology is subjected to a rigorous independent verification and validation process. This legislation is vital to restore accountability, but it is being held up for reasons unknown in the Senate, even though it passed unanimously in the House.

I am interested to hear from our witnesses on how CBP conducts market research, forges for emerging technology, repurposes existing Department of Defense equipment, and collaborates with DHS's Office of Science and Technology to mature technology not quite ready for field deployment. Congress repeatedly asked a very simple question when it comes to border security: What will it take to gain situational awareness and operational control of the Southern Border? Up until now, the answer we received have been limited, or not backed up by a requirements process, similar to what the Department of Defense uses. In short, it was a guess.

The Border Patrol and Air and Maritime Operations are involved in an effort called the "capability gap analysis process," or CGAP. It is an aerial-based exercise designed to ferret out tactical weaknesses in our border security defenses and, hopefully, inform the technological budget process. Congress expects the Border Patrol and Air and Marines to be able to quickly identify and justify the resources needed to secure the border. I am optimistic the CGAP process is a much-needed step in that direction.

Finding solutions to CBP's procurement woes and quickly meeting the technology requirements of the men and women charged with securing the border is the reason I am holding this hearing today. I look forward to the witnesses' testimony.

[The statement from Chairwoman McSally follows:]

STATEMENT OF CHAIRWOMAN MARTHA MCSALLY

MAY 24, 2016

The Southwest Border of the United States is home to nearly 2,000 miles of majestic, yet rugged and often treacherous terrain. Terrain that makes Border Patrol access, in some remote areas, a near impossible proposition.

Manpower alone, while essential, will never be enough to secure the border. In order to enhance situational awareness, we need to leverage technological force multipliers that provide surveillance across wide swaths of remote areas along the border.

Technologies such as cameras, night vision devices, motion sensors, and surveillance equipment, have become critical elements of our border security operations. These technologies have enhanced agent safety, provided constant monitoring of difficult to access areas, and extended situational awareness and the ability to interdict criminal activity.

Aviation assets, such as Unmanned Aerial Vehicles, equipped with advanced radar capabilities, have also refined our understanding of the significant threat that exists along the border and has helped reposition and redeploy assets as flow and vulnerabilities shift.

But technology cannot do any of those things if CBP's acquisition and procurement process cannot get these tools and the latest cutting-edge technology in the hands of the men and women on the ground in a timely fashion.

Situational awareness is contingent on feeding information from centralized operations centers, far from the border, down to the individual agent level, so they can respond accordingly. Technology has to be focused on meeting the immediate needs of the agent and not stove-piped in a command center.

CBP's border technology procurement efforts, to put it mildly, have a checkered history of not delivering timely acquisitions that include more failures than successes, including the Secure Border Initiative, Coastal Interceptor Vessel, Ultralight Aircraft Detection, and the Mobile Surveillance Capability, which have all become synonymous with a deeply-troubled acquisition process.

These procurements have run over budget, behind schedule, been subject to litigation, and wasted a good deal of taxpayer dollars to boot. In this time of limited budgets, we cannot afford to waste a billion dollars on a failed system to learn what not to do.

Border security cannot continue to be held back by a system that has an astonishing lack of urgency in getting it done for people on the ground.

Our agents and officers in the field desperately need the capabilities they have asked for to do the job, but on the whole, I do not believe that CBP's Office of Technology and Acquisition or (OTIA) has delivered.

OTIA's mission is to identify and acquire products and services to improve CBP's performance in securing the borders. OTIA has been the lead agency responsible for acquiring technologies associated with the Arizona Technology Plan.

But as far as I can tell, the only procurement that is working well and on budget is the Integrated Fixed Tower program, located principally in my district, however, this comes after chronic delays and the cancellation of SBInet. Now on track, Chief Vitiello recently certified to Congress that the program meets its operational requirements.

With the exception of that outlier, industry officials we have spoken to tell us over and over again that CBP's requirements are often poorly drafted, ill-defined and, perhaps most alarming, not stable.

Transparency is also a challenge, as is CBP's ability to forecast their needs so industry can spend the Research and Development dollars to mature technology for use in border security applications.

The Government Accountability Office has, on several occasions, criticized CBP for not following aspects of DHS's acquisition management guidance with the Arizona Border Technology plan, and the lack of performance metrics to determine if the cost is worth the border security improvement.

As a result of CBP's troubling procurement record, I authored the Border Security Technology Accountability Act that ensures border security programs are meeting cost, schedule, and performance thresholds and that technology is subjected to a rigorous independent verification and validation process.

This legislation is vital to restore accountability but is being held up, for reasons unknown, in the Senate.

I am interested to hear from our witnesses how CBP conducts market research, forages for emerging technology, repurposes excess Department of Defense equipment, and collaborates with DHS's office of Science and Technology to mature technology not quite ready for field deployment.

Congress repeatedly asks a very simple question when it comes to border security: What will it take to gain operational control and situational awareness of the Southern Border?

Up until now, the answer we received was limited, or not backed by a requirements process similar to what the Defense Department uses. In short, it was a guess.

The Border Patrol and Air and Marine Operations are involved in an effort called the Capability Gap Analysis Process, or C–GAP, a scenario-based exercise designed to ferret out tactical weaknesses in our border security defenses and hopefully inform the technological budget process.

Congress expects the Border Patrol and Air and Marine to be able to quickly identify, and justify the resource needs required to secure the border. I am optimistic that the C–GAP process is a much needed step in that direction.

Finding solutions to CBP's procurement woes and quickly meeting the technological requirements of the men and women charged with securing the border is the reason I am holding this hearing today.

I look forward to the witness's testimony.

Ms. MCSALLY. The Chair now recognizes the Ranking Member of the subcommittee, the gentleman from Texas, Mr. Vela, for a statement he might have.

Mr. VELA. Thank you, Madam Chairwoman. I am pleased to join you for today's hearing, examining U.S. Customs and Border Protection's efforts to enhance border security through the use of technology.

As a Member of Congress representing a district in the U.S.-Mexico border, I understand the importance of technology to achieving improved situational awareness, enhanced security, and improved facilitation of legitimate traffic along our Nation's borders.

The Department of Homeland Security has, for years, attempted to delay various kinds of technology to the borders with mixed results. To be fair, identifying, acquiring, and deploying the right mix of border security technology is no easy task. Technology evolves over time. The flow of border crosses and illicit traffic changes. America's borders are varied places with different geography, terrain, and climate, meaning that what works in Arizona may not work in South Texas, and likely will not work on our northern borders. It is important that this committee conduct careful oversight of CBP's on-going border security technology efforts, including the Arizona border surveillance technology plan, and deployment of integrated fixed towers in Arizona, procurement of mobile surveillance technologies, and the use of Predator B unmanned aircraft.

The Government Accountability Office has reported on the Arizona border surveillance technology plan identifying management, scheduling, and cost concerns similar to those that contributed to SBInet's problems.

I hope to hear from our GAO witness today about whether and how those issues are being addressed by CBP. Given my particular interest in South Texas, I also hope to hear from our witnesses about the border security's technologies in use or planned for the South Texas region. For example, I understand that there was a protest with a contract award for mobile video surveillance system units which consist of short- and medium-range mobile surveillance equipment mounted on telescoping masks mounted on Border Patrol vehicles. Many of the projected 297 units are slated for deployment in the Rio Grande Valley, and I hope to learn what the revised time line is for deployment.

I also know that the weather in Corpus Christi has proven challenging for flying CBP's Predator Bs prompting the agency to fly the aircraft from other locations.

I hope to hear from CBP about how these issues have affected situational awareness along the border in South Texas, if at all.

Finally, I hope we can have a frank discussion with our witnesses about how CBP can best position its on-going border security technology programs for success. I thank the witnesses for joining us today, and I yield back.

Ms. MCSALLY. The gentleman yields.

Other Members of the committee are reminded that opening statements may be submitted for the record.

[The statement of Ranking Member Thompson follows:]

STATEMENT OF RANKING MEMBER BENNIE G. THOMPSON

MAY 24, 2016

This committee has conducted vigorous oversight of DHS's attempts to deploy security technology along our Nation's borders over the years—and with good reason. Beginning with the Integrated Surveillance Intelligence System (ISIS), later the

America's Shield Initiative (ASI), and more recently Project 28 and SBInet, DHS has consistently over-promised and underdelivered border security technology.

For example, at the time then-Secretary Janet Napolitano canceled SBInet, the program had been deployed to only 53 miles of border in Arizona at a cost of about $1 BILLION. This committee has been fortunate to have the Government Accountability Office (GAO) engaged on each of these procurements, contributing significantly to our oversight efforts.

With respect to its on-going program, the Arizona Border Security Technology Plan, 2 years ago GAO reported that CBP was not following best practices for scheduling, verifying cost estimates with independent sources, testing technology to determine effectiveness and suitability, or establishing performance metrics for the technology. In short, GAO's initial work showed that the program suffers from some of the same deficiencies that ultimately led the Department to cancel the SBInet program.

In March of this year, GAO reported on CBP's Integrated Fixed Tower (IFT) acquisition, a key component of the Arizona Border Surveillance Technology Plan. Announced in March 2012, the IFTs—53 fixed surveillance tower units equipped with ground surveillance radar, infrared cameras, and communications systems—were intended to address the capability gap left when SBInet was canceled.

Unfortunately, DHS was forced to re-baseline the IFT program in December 2015, about 3 years after CBP determined the program could not meet its initial schedule goals. The program's full operational capability date has so far slipped from September 2015 to September 2020, and acquisition costs have increased by $53 million. Those of us who participated in SBInet oversight had hoped CBP learned its lessons from that program and would be applying them to this newer effort in Arizona.

I hope to hear from CBP and GAO today about the reasons for the cost, schedule, and performance changes for the IFTs. Similarly, I want to have a frank discussion about CBP's other major border security technology acquisitions and assets, including Mobile Surveillance Capabilities (MSCs), aerostats, and Predator Bs. I continue to support using technology as a force-multiplier along our Nation's borders.

However, if there is anything our oversight of DHS's efforts have shown, border security technology must be procured, deployed, and utilized in an appropriate, cost-effective manner. Otherwise, CBP could be left with yet another border security technology system that fails to deliver as promised.

Ms. McSALLY. We are pleased to be joined by 4 distinguished witnesses to discuss the important topic today:

Ronald Vitiello, the acting chief of the U.S. Border Patrol. As a chief operating officer, he is responsible for the daily operations of the U.S. Border Patrol and assist the commissioner of U.S. Customs and Border Protection in planning and directing Nation-wide enforcement. Chief Vitiello began his Border Patrol career in 1985, and has served in the Swanson, Tucson, and Laredo sectors.

Randolph Alles is the executive assistant commissioner for CBP's Office of Air and Marine, a position he has held since January 2013.

In this role, Mr. Alles is charged with overseeing the AMO mission of using aviation and maritime assets to detect, interdict, and prevent acts of terrorism, and the unlawful movement of drugs and other contraband from entering the United States.

Before joining the AMO, he spent 35 years in the United States Marine Corps—Semper Fi—retiring in 2011 as a major general.

Mark Borkowski became the assistant commissioner for the Office of Technology Innovation and Acquisition, or OTIA, at U.S. Customs and Border Protection, or CBP, in July 2010. In this role, he is responsible for ensuring technology efforts are properly focused on mission, and well-integrated across CBP. Prior to his appointment as assistant commissioner, Mr. Borkowski was the executive director of the Secure Border Initiative, SBI.

Rebecca Gambler is the director in the House U.S.—sorry. Let me do this again—is a director in the U.S. Government Accountability Office, Homeland Security and Justice team, where she leads GAO's work on border security, immigration, and the Department of Homeland Security's management and transformation. Prior to joining GAO, Ms. Gambler worked at the National Endowment for Democracy's International Forum or Democratic Studies.

The witnesses' full written statements will appear in the record. The Chair now recognizes Chief Vitiello for 5 minutes.

STATEMENT OF RONALD VITIELLO, ACTING CHIEF, U.S. BORDER PATROL, U.S. DEPARTMENT OF HOMELAND SECURITY

Mr. VITIELLO. Thank you, Chairwoman McSally, Ranking Member Vela, and distinguished Members of the subcommittee. It is an honor to appear before you today on behalf of the dedicated men and women of the United States Border Patrol, and discuss the role of technology in our border security operations between the ports of entry. This Saturday, the 28th, marks the Border Patrol's birthday. Since 1924, the men and women of this agency have made significant contributions to securing the homeland, from mounted watchmen riding the line in 1924; to guarding Nazi prisoners of war; in 1961, securing domestic air flights as marshals; and integrating universities in Oxford and Montgomery in 1962.

Proven to be a versatile and effective workforce, our agents have helped to capture escaped felons in New York in June of last year. On our borders, we try to innovate and use technology that enhances agent effectiveness and keeps them safe.

In 1935, we were advanced enough to install and use two-way radios in cars and stations. Today, the advanced technology deployed along our borders not only enhances the security of our Nation by providing us with increased situational awareness of illegal activity, it also significantly increases the safety of our front-line agents. While the basic Border Patrol mission is to secure the Nation's border from illegal entry of persons and goods has not changed in the past 92 years, the operational environment in which we work and the threats we face have changed significantly.

Today, our mission includes deterring acts of terrorism, detecting and intercepting human drug and weapon smuggling and trafficking, and preventing and responding to other criminal activity. The effective deployment of fixed and mobile technology is critical to the Border Patrol operations. With these resources, our front-line agents are better-informed, more effective, and safer. There is no doubt that technology is a critical factor of the Border Patrol strategic plan, which implements a security approach based on risk, and emphasizes unity of effort through integrated planning and execution with our partners.

Detection technology extends the visual range and awareness of front-line agents. Ground sensors alert agents to movements and activity, while mounted cameras and sensors on fixed—on aircraft fixed towers and Border Patrol vehicles can be controlled remotely to verify a target.

All of this technology works together, and ultimately enables the Border Patrol to gain situational awareness, direct a response team to the best interdiction location, and forewarn agents of any danger otherwise unknown along the way.

The Border Patrol continually evaluates our situational awareness posture, adjusts our capabilities as required to secure our borders. We work closely with our operational intelligence and acquisition colleagues within CBP and DHS to identify and develop technology, such as tunnel detection, and monitoring technology, small unmanned aircraft systems, tactical communication upgrades, and border surveillance tools tailored for the Southwest Border and northern borders.

In coordination with the DHS joint requirements process, the Border Patrol will continue to use the capability gap analysis process to conduct mission analysis and identify capability gaps and potential operational requirements over the short, medium, and long term.

With all our border technology, CBP works closely with agents on the ground to develop operational requirements, conduct testing and evaluation, and obtain user feedback to ensure the right tools are applied to the right capability gap.

Thank you, again, for the opportunity to discuss how technology enhances the Border Patrol's capabilities and strengthens our efforts in securing the border. I look forward to your questions.

Ms. McSALLY. Thank you, Mr. Vitiello.

The Chair now recognizes Major Alles for 5 minutes.

STATEMENT OF MAJOR GENERAL RANDOLPH D. "TEX" ALLES, (RET.–USMC), EXECUTIVE ASSISTANT COMMISSIONER, OFFICE OF AIR AND MARINE OPERATIONS, U.S. CUSTOMS AND BORDER PROTECTION, U.S. DEPARTMENT OF HOMELAND SECURITY

Mr. ALLES. Good afternoon, Chairwoman McSally and Ranking Member Vela and Members of the committee. It is an honor to appear before you today to discuss the critical role of technology, and specifically CPB's Air and Marine assets in securing our Nation's borders. CBP's Air and Marine Operations, or AMOs as we call ourselves is a critical component of the CBP's layered border security strategy. AMO's 1,272 law enforcement agents operate 243 aircraft and 360 vessels, and has sophisticated domain awareness network across the United States, Puerto Rico, and the Virgin Islands. AMO's critical aerial and maritime missions fall under 4 core competencies: Domain awareness, investigation, interdiction, and contingency operations and National taskings. AMO is a vital contributor to the security of our borders interdicting illicit traffic in the air, on the land, and the littoral waters of the United States through the coordinated use of integrated Air and Marine forces.

All our highly-specialized law enforcement agents provide unique expertise and capability domains in which we operate. Since the consolidation of Air and Marine assets within AMO 11 years ago, we have transformed from a force composed primarily of light observation aircraft into a modern air and maritime fleet equipped with sophisticated surveillance sensors and communication systems. We are working to increase the connectivity and networking among all our Air and Marine assets. AMO is continuing the efforts to reduce the number of our aircraft types and position our assets for highest utilization, which will increase both efficiency and effectiveness of our operations.

I would like to take this opportunity to highlight a few of our key assets and describe how this technology furthers CBP's capability to detect, identify, monitor, and appropriately respond to threats in our Nation's borders.

First, our multi-role enforcement aircraft are highly capable and equipped with sophisticated technology systems that enable it to be effective over both land and water. These aircraft are replacing several older single-mission assets and enhance CBP's interdiction and investigative capabilities.

Second, beyond our borders in the source and transit zone, CBP's P–3 long-range aircraft has been instrumental in countering narcotic operations, transnational criminal organizations, and vessels thousands of miles from the homeland. I might mention, they have just completed a rewinging of 14 aircraft, a $410 million program which came in under cost and ahead of schedule.

Third, in the maritime environment working in conjunction with the aviation assets, our new coastal interceptor vessels are physically designed and engineered with the speed maneuverability, integrity, and endurance to intercept and engage in a variety of suspect noncompliant vessels in offshore waters as well as the Great Lakes and on the Northern Border.

Finally, a vital component of our doing awareness is the Intermarine Operations Center. IMOC leverages advanced surveillance systems, integrates information from Federal, State, local, international, law enforcement, and intelligence sources to detect, identify, track, and direct the interdiction of suspect criminal use of noncommercial air and maritime conveyances approaching, crossing, or operating inside the United States—operating inside the borders of United States and Puerto Rico.

We work closely with our operation and acquisition colleagues at CBP, including the DHS Science and Technology Directorate to identify and develop surveillance and detection technology. AMO is also working with Domestic Nuclear Detection Office at DHS to develop and test radiological and nuclear detection threats beyond— threats aboard our small vessels.

Chairwoman McSally, and Ranking Member Vela, and distinguished Members of the committee, thank you for this opportunity to discuss AMO's technology assets, capabilities, and efforts in securing our borders. I look forward to your questions in a few moments. Thank you.

Ms. MCSALLY. Thank you, General Alles.

The Chair now recognizes Mr. Borkowski for 5 minutes.

STATEMENT OF MARK BORKOWSKI, ASSISTANT COMMISSIONER AND CHIEF ACQUISITION EXECUTIVE, OFFICE OF TECHNOLOGY INNOVATION AND ACQUISITION, U.S. CUSTOMS AND BORDER PROTECTION, U.S. DEPARTMENT OF HOMELAND SECURITY

Mr. BORKOWSKI. Thank you, Chairwoman McSally, Ranking Member Vela, and distinguished Members of the committee. It is a pleasure to be back before you.

As you suggested, Chairwoman McSally, it certainly has been a challenging few years, and I share your frustration with the delays.

The procurement system is very frustrating, I think, to all of us. I look forward to a discussion of that.

When I was last here before you 2 years ago, we were just getting to the point where we were awarding contracts, and in many cases, there were 2 years of delays in getting to those contract awards. A number of reasons for that, some of it is cultural, some of it is structural, but that has been a continuing frustration. However, since that time, actually, the performance on these contracts has been relatively good.

You cited the IFT, the Integrated Fixed Towers. As you may recall, that contract was awarded at a 75 percent cost savings compared to our original estimate and continues to perform consistently with that, and has performed pretty well against its schedule.

The remote video surveillance system is the other large significant program in Arizona. That program also has clicked along with—it was awarded at a reduced cost compared to our estimate. We have already deployed 4 AORs, the fifth will be completed by this year, and it has performed well on its cost.

The mobile surveillance capability is completely deployed to Arizona and is now extending its deployment outside of Arizona. That was awarded below its estimated cost and performed on cost. In addition, those systems have delivered on their performance.

So I think one of the things I would say is that is as an acquisition person, I essentially have 4 degrees of freedom that I play with: Cost, schedule, performance, and risk.

For the most part, I think we have not done well on schedule. I would have to acknowledge that. We have failed on schedule. We are trying to attack that. I am still looking for more ways to do that. But on the cost, schedule, and performance on these systems, I actually think we have done well once we got them going.

So Arizona is well under way compared to the baseline. The next area of emphasis on the Southwest Border has been Texas. Because of the money we saved, we were actually able to free up resources to do what our—they started out as pilots with DOD reuse, Department of Defense reuse systems. I think the most visible of those are the tactical aerostats. We now have 6 flying in Texas. We are putting up 17 of the towers that are associated with those—with cameras and potentially radars in areas that, frankly, would not have had technology until probably 2018, 2019 because we were able to generate savings, and by working with the Department of Defense, we are able to get a little more speed in delivery.

Having said that, though, that is not the long-term plan for Texas. The long-term plan for Texas has been remote video surveillance systems, mobile video surveillance systems. Those contracts are underway. The challenge in Texas has to do with environmental land clearances, land acquisition. Those are challenges. We are working through those, but that is an 18- to 24-month problem that we are working through.

We have gotten tremendous support from Congress on funding for that. We are working our way through that.

Sir, Congressman Vela, with respect to the mobile video surveillance systems, those are also, as you suggested, designated for Texas. They are very critical there.

The current contract will provide about 127 of those. The protest has been resolved in our favor. The contract is under way. We expect to deliver the first 4 of those toward the end of this year for testing, and then, over the next 2 years, deliver 127 that will be covered under the contract.

So I think we have made some progress. Am I completely satisfied? No. We do have some work to do in terms of, how do we handle this very, very slow acquisition process? How do we improve that? I look forward to discussions on that.

Having said that, I do think the programs that we have awarded have largely been successful once we have gotten over that procurement hump. I look forward to questions going forward.

[The joint prepared statement of Mr. Vitiello, Mr. Alles, and Mr. Borkowski follows:]

PREPARED STATEMENT OF RONALD VITIELLO, RANDOLPH D. "TEX" ALLES, AND MARK BORKOWSKI

MAY 24, 2016

Chairwoman McSally, Ranking Member Vela, and distinguished Members of the committee. It is a pleasure to appear before you today on behalf of U.S. Customs and Border Protection (CBP) to discuss the acquisition and deployment of border security technology between our Nation's ports of entry (POE).

Along the more than 5,000 miles of border with Canada, 1,900 miles of border with Mexico, and approximately 95,000 miles of shoreline, CBP secures our borders and associated airspace and maritime approaches to prevent illegal entry of people and goods into the United States. The border environment in which CBP works is dynamic and requires continual adaptation to respond to emerging threats and changing conditions. We appreciate the partnership and support we have received from this committee, whose commitment to the security of the American people has enabled the continued deployment of advanced technology assets needed to secure the border.

In the acquisition and deployment of border security technology, CBP ensures that investments are effective and that procurement processes are efficient, transparent, and compliant with Federal law and Department of Homeland Security (DHS) policy. With all our programs, operations, and activities, we welcome oversight and embrace our responsibility as stewards of American taxpayer resources.

When CBP was formed in 2003, it was an organization comprised of components that had different approaches, methods, and policies regarding acquisition and management activities. Although our operations had been integrated under one mission, CBP, and in a broader context DHS, lacked a standardized and unified acquisition structure, including governance and oversight, strong requirements development process, and centralized resource allocation. In order to strengthen and streamline acquisition management throughout the Department, Secretary Johnson launched the Unity of Effort initiative, which established a more collaborative process for decision making, including those that shape acquisition and resource allocation.

A key element of the Unity of Effort initiative is the establishment of the Joint Requirements Council (JRC), designed to improve the quality and validity of the Department's requirements generation and oversight process. The JRC creates a stronger focus earlier in the investment life cycle—at the requirements development stage—to better position DHS components, including CBP, to effectively and efficiently execute acquisition strategies and budgets that ultimately close capability gaps.

As part of this initiative, CBP is the sponsoring component for DHS Joint Task Force West and a participating component in Joint Task Force East and Joint Task Force for Investigations. These Joint Task Forces are conducting the DHS Southern Border and Approaches Campaign Plan (SBAC), launched in early 2015, which put the assets and personnel of the Department to use in a combined and strategic way to collaboratively plan and execute multi-component DHS operations to better protect the border. Aimed at leveraging the range of unique Department roles, responsibilities, and capabilities, the Campaign enhances our operational capability to address comprehensive threat environments in a unified way. Together, the DHS Unity of Effort initiative and the Campaign will drive border security investments and direct DHS resources in a much more collaborative fashion to address the range of threats and challenges, including illegal migration, smuggling of illegal drugs, human and arms trafficking, the illicit financing of such operations, and threat of terrorist exploitation of border vulnerabilities.

Our testimony today will discuss CBP's technology investments between the POEs, highlight some of CBP's deployed border technology assets, and describe the agency's path forward to ensure that CBP's acquisition strategies and structure is in place to meet the challenge of a dynamic border threat environment.

TECHNOLOGY INVESTMENTS BETWEEN PORTS OF ENTRY

For CBP, the use of technology in the border environment is an invaluable force multiplier to increase situational awareness. Thanks to the support of Congress, CBP continues to deploy proven, effective technology to strengthen border security operations between the POEs—in the land, air, and maritime environments. With enhanced surveillance capabilities, CBP can improve its situational awareness remotely, direct a response team to the best interdiction location, and warn the team of any additional danger otherwise unknown along the way. As a result, these investments increase CBP's visibility on the border, operational capabilities, and the safety of front-line law enforcement personnel.

It is imperative that DHS and CBP promote operational agility by leveraging technological advances and innovative practices. A key element of CBP's acquisition strategy, innovation is not simply the process of buying the newest technology; rather, it is the product of a collaborative culture that supports creativity, optimizes resource allocation and pursues the greatest return on investment and delivery of prioritized operational capabilities.

This committee is familiar with the outcome of CBP's SBInet program, an earlier component of the DHS Secure Border Initiative (SBI) that was designed as a comprehensive and integrated technology program to provide persistent surveillance across U.S. borders. The program experienced significant schedule delays and cost overruns because it did not allow necessary flexibility to adapt to differing needs in the various regions of the border. SBInet eventually delivered systems to 2 Areas of Responsibility (AORs) in Arizona that continue to operate successfully. Nevertheless, DHS cancelled SBInet on January 14, 2011, because it was too costly and the idea of one, all-encompassing program was unnecessarily complex for border technology.

Since 2011, DHS and CBP have approached our border technology requirements, ranging from small to large, simple to complex, in more manageable pieces tailored to specific regions on the border. For example, CBP's Arizona Technology Plan (ATP), which focuses on technology that specifically meets the needs of border conditions in Arizona, is the first of many phases in a multi-year effort to provide a cost-effective mix of fixed and mobile technology across the Southwest Border. The ATP acquisition strategy leverages "non-developmental" technology to the greatest extent possible, providing more flexible, less risky, and less costly procurements and deployments. Using the non-developmental approach, most of the programs within the ATP are on contract and many systems have already been deployed. Although it is too early to declare complete success, the early indications of the acquisition strategy are quite positive and, in some cases, far exceed our expectations.

There is no one-size-fits-all approach to border security technology acquisition. CBP's Office of Technology Innovation and Acquisition (OTIA) works collaboratively with the U.S. Border Patrol (USBP) and Air and Marine Operations (AMO) to develop requirements, test and evaluate technology, and deploy effective technology in support of CBP's border security mission.

Fixed, Persistent Surveillance

Integrated Fixed Tower (IFT) systems are one of the technologies that are in the process of being acquired and deployed to the Southwest Border in Arizona as part of the ATP. IFTs are fixed surveillance assets that provide long-range persistent surveillance. These systems cover very large areas and incorporate a Common Operating Picture (COP), a central hub that receives data from one or multiple tower units. The tower systems automatically detect and track items of interest, and provide the COP operator(s) with the data, video, and geospatial location of selected items of interest to identify and classify them. In February of this year, the USBP conditionally accepted the IFT system and is currently looking to develop improvements for the already-deployed system.

Remote Video Surveillance Systems (RVSS) are another fixed technology asset used in select areas along the Southwest and Northern borders. These systems provide short-, medium-, and long-range persistent surveillance mounted on stand-alone towers, or other structures. The RVSS uses cameras, radio, and microwave transmitters to send video to a control room and enables a control room operator to remotely detect, identify, classify, and track targets using the video feed.

Without fixed-system technology such as IFT and RVSS, the Border Patrol's ability to detect, identify, classify, and track illicit activity would be decreased. Fixed systems provide line-of-sight surveillance coverage to efficiently detect incursions in flat terrain. The Border Patrol integrates mobile and portable systems to address areas where rugged terrain and dense ground cover may allow adversaries to penetrate through blind spots or avoid the coverage areas of fixed systems.

Mobile Capabilities

The border environment between the ports of entry is dynamic. Working in conjunction with fixed surveillance assets, CBP's mobile technology assets provide flexibility and agility to adapt to changing border conditions and threats. Mobile technologies are deployed in California, Arizona, New Mexico, and Texas as well as several Northern Border locations. Along the Southwest Border, Mobile Surveillance Capability (MSC) systems provide long-range mobile surveillance and consist of a suite of radar and camera sensors mounted on Border Patrol vehicles. An agent deploys with the vehicle to operate the system, which automatically detects and tracks items of interest and provides the agent/operator with data and video of the observed subject.

Mobile Vehicle Surveillance Systems (MVSS) provide short- and medium-range mobile surveillance equipment mounted on telescoping masts and consist of a suite of camera sensors mounted on Border Patrol vehicles. An agent deploys with the system, which detects, tracks, identifies, and classifies items of interest using the video feed. The agent/operator observes activity on the video monitor to detect intrusions and assist agents/officers in responding to those intrusions.

Another system, which does not need to be mounted to a vehicle, is the Agent Portable Surveillance System (APSS). These systems provide medium-range mobile surveillance, and are transported by 2 or 3 agents and mounted on a tripod. Two agents remain on-site, one to operate the system, which automatically detects and tracks items of interest and provides the agent/operator with data and video of selected items of interest.

In some areas along the Southwest Border, CBP also uses Unattended Ground Sensors (UGS), which provide short-range persistent surveillance. These sensors support our capability to detect, and to a limited extent, track, and identify subjects. Sensor capabilities include seismic, passive infrared, acoustic, contact closure, and magnetic, although these capabilities are not necessarily available in all deployed UGS. When a ground sensor is activated, an alarm is communicated to a data decoder that translates the sensor's activation data to a centralized computer system in an operations center. Some UGS are used in conjunction with Imaging Sensors (IS). The UGS/IS include an imaging capability to transmit images or video back to the operations center. As with UGS, UGS/IS are monitored in a centralized system and geospatially tracked.

CBP's Tactical Aerostats and Re-locatable Towers program, originally part of the Department of Defense (DOD) Re-use program, uses a mix of aerostats, towers, cameras, and radars to provide Border Patrol with increased situational awareness through an advanced surveillance capability over a wide area. This capability has proven to be a vital asset in increasing CBP's ability to detect, identify, classify, and track activity.

The absence of mobile surveillance technology would limit the Border Patrol's ability to detect, identify, classify, track, and rapidly respond to illicit activity. These technologies not only provide significant security benefits and multiply the capabilities of law enforcement personnel to detect, identify, and respond to suspicious activity, but they also assist with public safety along the border. Mobile surveillance technology systems enable agents to position the technology where it is needed at a specific moment, extend our observational capabilities, and increase the accuracy and speed of our response.

Technology is critical to border security operations. A tailored blend of fixed, mobile, and portable surveillance systems that complement one another increases the Border Patrol's effectiveness in targeting a response to high-risk areas, enabling rapid response strategies to maximize limited manpower, and adjusting to seasonal/ periodic traffic patterns.

Air and Marine Capabilities

AMO increases CBP's situational awareness, enhances its detection and interdiction capabilities, and extends our border security zones, offering greater capacity to stop threats prior to reaching the Nation's shores. Through the use of coordinated and integrated surveillance capabilities—including aviation, marine, tethered aerostats, and integrated ground-based radars—AMO detects, interdicts, and prevents acts of terrorism and the unlawful movement of people, illegal drugs, and other contraband toward or across the borders of the United States. These assets provide multi-domain awareness for our partners across the Department, as well as critical aerial and maritime surveillance, interdiction, and operational assistance to our ground personnel.

AMO's maritime assets are tailored to the conditions of the threat environment in which we operate, and equipped with the capabilities required to interdict attempted illicit smuggling of drugs and undocumented aliens. Often there is little time to interdict inbound suspect vessels and AMO has honed its maritime border security response capability around rapid and effective interception, pursuit, and interdiction of these craft. AMO employs high-speed Coastal Interceptor Vessels (CIV) that are specifically designed and engineered with the speed, maneuverability, integrity, and endurance to intercept and engage a variety of suspect non-compliant vessels in offshore waters, as well as the Great Lakes on the Northern Border.

CBP's aerial surveillance capabilities are enhanced through recent investments and deployments of Multi-Role Enforcement Aircraft (MEA). The MEA has a multi-mode radar for use over water and land, an electro-optical/infrared camera system, and a satellite communications system. The MEA replaces several older, single-mission assets and remains the only asset customized to provide maritime support in the near-shore customs waters. With its sophisticated technology systems, the MEA is a highly capable, twin-engine aircraft and a critical investment in CBP's maritime, land, and aerial surveillance capabilities.

P–3 Long-Range Trackers and Airborne Early Warning Aircraft provide critical detection and interdiction capability in both the air and marine environment. Sophisticated sensors and high-endurance capability greatly increase CBP's range to counter illicit trafficking. AMO P–3s are an integral part of the successful counter-narcotic missions operating in coordination with the Joint Interagency Task Force—South. The P–3s patrol in a 42-million-square-mile area that includes more than 41 nations, the Pacific Ocean, Gulf of Mexico, Caribbean Sea, and seaboard approaches to the United States. In fiscal year 2015, CBP's P–3s operational efforts led to the total seizure or disruption of more than 204,464 pounds of cocaine with an estimated street value of $15.3 billion.

Another important asset is the DHC–8 Maritime Patrol Aircraft (MPA). It bridges the gap between the strategic P–3 and Unmanned Aircraft System (UAS) assets and the smaller assets providing support in the littoral waters. This tool allows AMO an unprecedented level of situational awareness in the Gulf of Mexico and the Caribbean.

AMO's tactical resources have also received a number of technological upgrades to add to their utility. The AS–350 helicopter has received avionics upgrades to allow the operators to focus more of their attention on the mission, making them more effective. AMO has also added detection technology to its fixed-wing light observation aircraft, greatly increasing its tactical capabilities.

Additionally, UAS are increasingly instrumental in CBP's layered and integrated approach to border security. The UAS consists of an unmanned aircraft, sensors, communication packages, pilots, and ground control operators. UAS are used to meet surveillance and other mission requirements along the Southwest Border, Northern Border, Southeast coastal area, and in the drug source and transit zones. Four of CBP's UAS are equipped with Vehicle and Dismount Exploitation Radar (VADER) sensor systems, which are capable of detecting human movement along the ground and increase CBP aerial surveillance, enforcement, and security to prevent potential threats from illegally entering the United States. Since 2012, VADER has detected over 40,000 people moving across the Southwest Border. Since 2006, this versatile platform has been credited with interdicting/disrupting 13,144 pounds of cocaine and 321,330 pounds of marijuana worth an estimated $1.8 billion. The UAS program has achieved over 35,900 flight hours since program inception in fiscal year 2006.

UAS and P–3 aircraft are equipped with technology that provides full-motion video capture and provides real-time and forensic analysis. This advanced detection and communication system enables CBP to disseminate images and other sensor data to operational users in real time, increasing response effectiveness and speed.

Perhaps the most important advancements come in the area of data integration and exploitation. Downlink technology, paired with the BigPipe system, allows AMO to provide a video feed and situational awareness to its law enforcement partners in real time. In addition, the Minotaur mission integration system will allow multiple aircraft to share information from multiple sources, providing a never-before-seen level of air, land, and sea domain awareness. As the Minotaur system evolves, it will provide even greater awareness for a greater number of users.

AMO also combats airborne and maritime smuggling with an integrated long-range radar architecture comprised of ground-based radars and elevated radars deployed on tethered aerostats. AMO, in partnership with DOD, operates and maintains a large network of terrestrial radars to establish and maintain wide-area, persistent surveillance of commercial and non-commercial aircraft flying toward, arriving at, or passing through our borders. With the awareness generated by this sensor network, CBP can detect and respond to air and maritime movement anomalies that could pose a threat to our homeland, including trafficking organizations attempting to deliver contraband across the border by flying beneath the radar field of view of our ground-based radars.

AMO's Tethered Aerostat Radar System (TARS) monitors the low-altitude approaches to the United States and denies this airspace for illicit smuggling. With 8 aerostat sites—6 along the Southwest Border, 1 in the Florida Keys, and 1 in Puerto Rico—the TARS' elevated sensor mitigates the effect of the curvature of the earth and terrain-masking limitations associated with ground-based radars, enabling maximum long-range radar detection capabilities. In fiscal years 2014 and 2015 TARS recorded nearly 1,000 suspected cross-border attempts, approximately 85 percent of all Southwest Border radar detections.

A vital component of DHS's domain awareness capabilities, CBP's Air and Marine Operations Center (AMOC) integrates surveillance capabilities and coordinates with other CBP operational components, including the USBP, Federal, and international partners[1] to detect, identify, track, and support interdiction of suspect aviation and maritime activity in the approaches to U.S. borders, at the borders, and within the interior of the United States. Coordinating with extensive law enforcement and intelligence databases and communication networks, AMOC's command-and-control operational system, the Air and Marine Operations Surveillance System (AMOSS), provides a single display that is capable of processing up to 700 individual sensor feeds and tracking over 50,000 individual targets simultaneously. The 8 TARS sites represent approximately 2 percent of the total available radars in AMOSS, yet were able to account for detecting 53 percent of all suspect target detections.

As we continue to deploy border surveillance technology, particularly along the Southwest Border, these investments in fixed and mobile technology, as well as enhancements of domain awareness capabilities provided by the AMOC allow CBP the flexibility to shift more officers and agents from detection duties to interdiction of illegal activities on our borders.

CBP'S ACQUISITION STRATEGY AND REALIGNMENT

Since its establishment in 2010, OTIA has led CBP's acquisition oversight and coordination efforts and has been recognized as the primary point of contact for CBP acquisition activities. While CBP's intent was for all mission offices' acquisition program management, requirement development, and oversight to be integrated and consolidated under OTIA, because of the broad scope of CBP's mission and diversity of operating environments, the management of several of CBP's large acquisition programs were not migrated to OTIA. However, in the past 5 years, OTIA has aligned CBP's acquisition policies, procedures, and practices with DHS Department standards, consolidated CBP's acquisition governance and accountability structure, brought multiple high-impact programs back on track, and has contracted, deployed and sustained critical border security technology assets.

In 2015, as part of on-going headquarters realignment efforts, CBP Commissioner R. Gil Kerlikowske engaged the Defense Acquisition University (DAU) to provide a review and recommendations of the state of CBP acquisition management. The key DAU alignment-related findings and recommendations included clarifying and strengthening the Component Acquisition Executive (CAE) independent oversight authority on behalf of the Commissioner; separating OTIA's key roles of oversight, requirements, and program management; and aligning programs and accountability with operational offices. To ensure that these recommended improvements are possible, and to ensure CBP's acquisition construct aligns with the DHS acquisition oversight framework, CBP is in the process of redirecting acquisition, program, and requirements management responsibilities.

This realignment is the next step forward in building off the achievements OTIA has made possible, including the standardization of acquisition policies, processes, and oversight and the development of acquisition expertise in the CBP workforce. The separation and redistribution of CBP's acquisition functions—including require-

---

[1] AMOC partners include the Federal Aviation Administration (FAA), the Department of Defense (including the North American Aerospace Defense Command (NORAD)), and the governments of Mexico, Canada, and the Bahamas.

ments development and program management—from OTIA to other areas within CBP's operational structure, increases acquisition effectiveness and efficiency, and strengthens agency oversight of acquisition activities. CBP's requirements function will be managed under the Operational Support (OS) division, where technical experts will work directly with front-line operators in the execution of a holistic, strategy-led requirements development program. The execution of acquisition programs will be aligned directly under CBP's operational components—USBP, AMO, and the Office of Field Operations—to tighten the link between acquisition programs, users, and funding. Acquisition program oversight, policy and procedures promulgation, and acquisition workforce management—under the leadership of the Chief Acquisition Officer—will be part of CBP's Enterprise Services (ES) division to create an even stronger alignment with the DHS acquisition framework. The realignment will result in stronger management much earlier in the acquisition investment life cycle, increased oversight, as well as better integration of CBP personnel and operational expertise.

CBP works closely with other elements of DHS headquarters and fellow Department components to ensure strategy-led, operationally-informed requirements development. In coordination with the DHS joint requirements process, the USBP and AMO will continue to use the Capability Gap Analysis Process (CGAP) to conduct mission analysis and identify capability gaps. From this analysis, OS will work with USBP and AMO to identify and plan operational requirements over the short-, mid-, and long-term and to identify potential solutions, which may (or may not) include fencing, roads, or other solutions depending on the nature, scope, severity, and geographic location of a given capability gap. AMO began C–GAP in October 2015 using best practices and lessons learned from the USBP process. The AMO process examines aviation and maritime mission spaces and capabilities, while taking advantage of the analytical models and processes the USBP has established. AMO and USBP gap analyses inform the OS-led requirements process and are prioritized and linked to Department activities and strategies. With all technology, CBP works closely with agents on the ground to develop operational requirements, conduct testing and evaluation, and obtain user feedback to ensure that the right tool is applied to the right capability gap. Terrain, threat, socio-economic, and political considerations vary greatly across sectors and regions, making a "one size fits all" approach ineffective.

CBP works closely with the DHS Science & Technology (S&T) Directorate to identify and develop technology to improve our surveillance and detection capabilities along our land and maritime borders. This includes investments in tunnel detection and tunnel activity monitoring technology; tactical communication upgrades, Small Unmanned Aircraft Systems (SUAS); low-flying aircraft detection and tracking systems, land and maritime data integration/data fusion capabilities, and border surveillance tools tailored to the Southwest and Northern Border, including unattended ground sensors/tripwires, upgrades for mobile Surveillance Systems, slash camera poles, and wide-area surveillance.

In addition to collaboration with our DHS partners, as part of CBP's efforts to seek innovative ways to acquire and use technology, CBP formed a partnership with DOD to identify and reuse excess DOD technology. To date, CBP has acquired several types of technology, including thermal imaging equipment, night vision equipment, and tactical aerostat systems, which increase CBP's situational awareness and operational flexibility in responding to border threats. We will continue to pursue additional opportunities to leverage DOD excess equipment. We will do this in a sustainable way by considering the full life-cycle costs of the DOD equipment we are considering before acquiring it.

CONCLUSION

Technology is a primary driver of all land, maritime, and air domain awareness. The information obtained from fixed and mobile surveillance systems, ground sensors, imaging systems, and other advanced technologies enhances domain awareness, informs situational awareness, and better enables CBP to monitor, detect, identify, and appropriately respond to threats in the Nation's border regions.

As we look to sustain and recapitalize our border security technology assets, we will look to the DHS joint requirement process to validate our mission requirements and the strengthened DHS budget and acquisition processes to ensure we have the funding and sustainment to operate existing equipment to maximum capacity and that we receive new assets with the capabilities we require on time and on budget.

While there is always more work to do, CBP has made significant strides to improve acquisition planning, management, and execution. These efforts have produced more effective governance and significant improvements to current and future acquisitions. Going forward, CBP will work with its DHS management partners to improve oversight; develop and increase our acquisition workforce; and improve the quality, timeliness, and transparency of CBP contracting processes.

Knit together by the DHS SBAC and the joint requirements processes, CBP's acquisition and rapid deployment of technology allows us to achieve our strategic and operational objectives in effectively and efficiently securing U.S. borders and the approaches.

Chairwoman McSally, Ranking Member Vela, thank you for the opportunity to testify today. We look forward to your questions.

Ms. MCSALLY. Thank you, Mr. Borkowski.

The Chair now recognizes Ms. Gambler for 5 minutes.

STATEMENT OF REBECCA GAMBLER, DIRECTOR, HOMELAND SECURITY AND JUSTICE, U.S. GOVERNMENT ACCOUNTABILITY OFFICE

Ms. GAMBLER. Good afternoon, Chairwoman McSally, Ranking Member Vela, and Members of the subcommittee. I appreciate the opportunity to testify at today's hearing to discuss GAO's work reviewing DHS's efforts to acquire and deploy various technologies and other assets along U.S. borders. DHS has employed a variety of assets in its efforts to secure the Southwest Border, including various land-based surveillance technologies, unmanned aerial systems, or UAS, and tactical aerostats.

My remarks today will summarize some of GAO's past work on management and oversight of various surveillance technologies. I will also share some preliminary observations from our on-going work for this subcommittee reviewing CBP's use of UAS and tactical aerostats.

First, GAO has issued numerous reports on DHS's efforts to plan for, deploy, and manage land-based surveillance technologies under the former Secure Border Initiative and the current Arizona Border Surveillance Technology Plan.

CBP has made progress in deploying programs under the plan, including fixed and mobile surveillance systems, agent portable devices, and ground sensors, and these technologies have aided CBP's border security efforts. However, we have also reported that CBP could do more to strengthen its management of the plan and technology programs and better assess the contributions of surveillance technologies to apprehensions and seizures.

For example, CBP has previously experienced delays in some of its surveillance technology programs, and CBP's planned dates for initial and full operational capability for the Integrated Fixed Towers, for example, have slipped by several years.

We have previously reviewed CBP's schedules and life-cycle cost estimates for the highest-cost programs under the plan, and compared them to best practices. Overall, the schedules and estimates for the plans programs reflected some, but not all best practices, and we found that CBP could take further action to better ensure the reliability of its schedules and cost estimates by more fully applying those best practices.

CBP has taken steps towards addressing our recommendations in these areas, such as recently providing us with updated schedules for some of the planned programs, and we will be reviewing them going forward to determine the extent to which they address our recommendation.

Further, CBP has identified the mission benefits of its surveillance technologies such as improved situational awareness and agent safety. CBP has also begun requiring Border Patrol to record data within its database on whether or not an asset, such as a camera, assisted in apprehension or seizure. These are positive steps toward helping CBP assess the contributions of its surveillance technologies to border security. However, CBP needs to develop and implement performance measures and analyzing data it is now collecting to be able to fully assess the contributions of its technologies to border security.

Second, with regard to UAS and tactical aerostats, based on our on-going work for the subcommittee, CBP is currently operating 9 Predator B aircraft from 4 locations across the country. These aircraft may be equipped with video and radar sensors, and they are used for a variety of functions, including patrol missions to support Border Patrol and other law enforcement agencies and to monitor natural disasters, like wildfires or floods.

CBP operates the aircraft in designated airspace, and more than 80 percent of flight hours from fiscal years 2011 to 2015 were associated with designated air space along border and coastal areas.

CBP also operates 6 tactical aerostats along the border in South Texas, as Mr. Borkowski mentioned, and these aerostats assist Border Patrol in apprehension and seizures.

CBP's use of both UAS and tactical aerostat can be affected by various factors, such as airspace access and weather.

In closing, we are continuing to examine CBP's use of UAS, tactical aerostats, and other assets and technologies as part of our ongoing work. We will also continue to follow up on actions taken by CBP in response to our recommendations for improving management and measurement of technologies deployed under the Arizona Border Surveillance Technology Plan,

This concludes my oral statement, and I am happy to answer any questions Members may have.

[The prepared statement of Ms. Gambler follows:]

PREPARED STATEMENT OF REBECCA GAMBLER

MAY 24, 2016

GAO HIGHLIGHTS

Highlights of GAO–16–671T, a testimony before the Subcommittee on Border and Maritime Security, Committee on Homeland Security, House of Representatives.

Why GAO Did This Study

CBP employs surveillance technologies, UAS, and other assets to help secure the border. For example, in January 2011, CBP developed the Arizona Border Surveillance Technology Plan, which includes 7 acquisition programs related to fixed and mobile surveillance systems, among other assets. CBP has also deployed UAS, including Predator B aircraft, as well as tactical aerostats to help secure the border. In recent years, GAO has reported on a variety of CBP border security programs and operations.

This statement addresses: (1) GAO findings on DHS's efforts to implement the Arizona Border Surveillance Technology Plan and (2) preliminary observations related to GAO's on-going work on CBP's use of UAS and tactical aerostats for border security. This statement is based on GAO products issued from November 2011 through April 2016, along with selected updates conducted in May 2016. For on-going work related to UAS, GAO reviewed CBP documents and analyzed Predator B flight-hour data from fiscal years 2011 through 2015, the time period when all Predator B centers became operational. GAO also conducted site visits in Texas and Arizona to view operation of Predator B aircraft and tactical aerostats and interviewed CBP officials responsible for these operations.

What GAO Recommends

GAO has previously made recommendations to DHS to improve its management of plans and programs for surveillance technologies and DHS generally agreed.

BORDER SECURITY.—DHS SURVEILLANCE TECHNOLOGY, UNMANNED AERIAL SYSTEMS AND OTHER ASSETS

What GAO Found

GAO reported in March 2014 and April 2015 that U.S. Customs and Border Protection (CBP), within the Department of Homeland Security (DHS), had made progress in deploying programs under the Arizona Border Surveillance Technology Plan (the Plan), but could take additional actions to strengthen its management of the Plan and its related programs. Specifically, in March 2014 GAO reported that CBP's schedules and life-cycle cost estimates for the Plan and its 3 highest-cost programs—which represented 97 percent of the Plan's total estimated cost—met some but not all best practices. GAO recommended that CBP ensure that its schedules and cost estimates more fully address best practices, such as validating cost estimates with independent estimates, and DHS concurred. As of May 2016, CBP has initiated or completed deployment of technology for each of the 3 highest-cost programs under the Plan, and reported updating some program schedules and cost estimates. For example, in May 2016, CBP provided GAO with complete schedules for 2 of the programs, and GAO will be reviewing them to determine the extent to which they address GAO's recommendation. GAO also reported in March 2014 that CBP had identified mission benefits of technologies under the Plan, such as improved situational awareness, but had not developed key attributes for performance metrics for all technologies, as GAO recommended in November 2011. As of May 2015, CBP had identified a set of potential key attributes for performance metrics for deployed technologies and expected to complete its development of baselines for measures by the end of 2015. In March 2016, GAO reported that CBP was adjusting the completion date to incorporate pending test and evaluation results for recently-deployed technologies under the Plan.

GAO's on-going work on CBP's use of unmanned aerial systems (UAS) for border security shows that CBP operates 9 Predator B aircraft in U.S. airspace in accordance with Federal Aviation Administration (FAA) requirements. Specifically, CBP's Air and Marine Operations operates the aircraft in accordance with FAA certificates of waiver or authorization for a variety of activities, such as training flights and patrol missions to support the U.S. Border Patrol's (Border Patrol) efforts to detect and apprehend individuals illegally crossing into the United States between ports of entry. Predator B aircraft are currently equipped with a combination of video and radar sensors that provide information on cross-border illegal activities to supported agencies. CBP data show that over 80 percent of Predator B flight hours were in airspace encompassing border and coastal areas from fiscal years 2011 through 2015. CBP officials stated that airspace access and hazardous weather can affect CBP's ability to utilize Predator B aircraft for border security activities. GAO's on-going work shows that CBP has deployed 6 tactical aerostats—relocatable unmanned buoyant craft tethered to the ground and equipped with cameras for capturing full-motion video—along the U.S.-Mexico border in south Texas to support Border Patrol. CBP operates 3 types of tactical aerostats, which vary in size and altitude of operation. CBP officials reported that airspace access, hazardous weather, and real estate (e.g., access to private property) can affect CBP's ability to deploy and utilize tactical aerostats. Border Patrol has taken actions to track the contribution of tactical aerostats to its mission activities.

Chairwoman McSally, Ranking Member Vela, and Members of the subcommittee: I am pleased to be here today to discuss the Department of Homeland Security's (DHS) efforts to acquire and deploy various technology and assets to secure U.S. borders. Within DHS, U.S. Customs and Border Protection's (CBP) U.S. Border Patrol (Border Patrol) is the Federal agency with primary responsibility for securing the National borders between U.S. ports of entry (POE).[1] CBP's Air and Marine Operations (AMO) has primary responsibility for detecting, interdicting, and preventing acts of terrorism and the unlawful movement of people, illegal drugs, and

---

[1] Ports of entry are facilities that provide for the controlled entry into or departure from the United States. Specifically, a port of entry is any officially designated location (seaport, airport, or land border location) where DHS officers or employees are assigned to clear passengers and merchandise, collect duties, and enforce customs laws, and where DHS officers inspect persons applying for admission into the United States pursuant to U.S. immigration law.

other contraband toward or across U.S. borders utilizing aviation and maritime assets. In the last 3 fiscal years, over 70 percent of all annual apprehensions of illegal entrants by Border Patrol have occurred along the Arizona and south Texas borders.[2] Seizures of marijuana and cocaine (in pounds) along the Arizona and south Texas borders reported by Border Patrol, as a percentage of all annual seizures, has ranged between 88 to 91 and 24 to 55 percent over the last 3 years, respectively.[3]

DHS has employed a variety of technology and assets to assist with its efforts to secure the border. For example, in November 2005, DHS announced the launch of the Secure Border Initiative (SBI) program, which was responsible for developing a comprehensive border protection system using technology, known as the Secure Border Initiative Network (SBInet). In January 2011, in response to internal and external assessments that identified concerns regarding the performance, cost, and schedule for implementing the systems, the Secretary of Homeland Security announced the cancellation of further procurements of SBInet systems. After the cancellation of SBInet, CBP developed the Arizona Border Surveillance Technology Plan (the Plan), in January 2011, which includes a mix of radars, sensors, and cameras to help provide security for the Arizona border to support Border Patrol. Additionally, AMO operates a fleet of air and marine assets in support of Federal border security efforts, including surveillance through Predator B unmanned aerial systems (UAS).[4] CBP also operates tactical aerostats along the border, which are relocatable unmanned buoyant craft tethered to the ground and equipped with surveillance technologies.

Over the years, we have reported on the progress and challenges DHS faces in implementing its border security efforts. My statement discusses our findings on: (1) DHS's efforts to implement the Arizona Border Surveillance Technology Plan and (2) preliminary observations related to our on-going work for this subcommittee on the use of UAS and tactical aerostats for border security.

This statement is based on reports and testimonies we issued from 2011 through April 2016 that examined DHS efforts to secure the U.S. border. It also includes selected updates we conducted in May 2016 on DHS's efforts to address our previous recommendations related to its Arizona Border Surveillance Technology Plan. Our reports and testimonies incorporated information we obtained and analyzed from officials from various DHS components. More detailed information about our scope and methodology can be found in our reports and testimonies. For the updates on our Arizona Border Surveillance Technology Plan work, we reviewed documents from DHS on actions it has taken to address findings and recommendations made in our prior reports on which this statement is based.

For on-going work related to UAS, we analyzed CBP policies, reports, requirements, and Predator B flight-hour data from fiscal year 2011 through 2015, covering the time period when all Predator B centers became operational. We also interviewed CBP officials responsible for Predator B and tactical aerostat operations. To assess the reliability of Predator B flight hour data, we reviewed guidance for reporting flight hours, interviewed CBP officials about their policies and procedures related to tracking flight hours, and compared monthly report data with data from other CBP flight hour reports. We found the data were sufficiently reliable for the purposes of reporting how CBP allocates its Predator B flight hours. As part of our on-going work, we also conducted site visits to Arizona in February 2016 and south Texas in March 2016 where we observed Predator B and tactical aerostat operations and interviewed CBP officials that operate and utilize these assets.

We conducted our past and on-going work in accordance with generally accepted Government auditing standards. Those standards require that we plan and perform the audit to obtain sufficient, appropriate evidence to provide a reasonable basis for our findings and conclusions based on our audit objectives. We believe that the evidence obtained provides a reasonable basis for our findings and conclusions based on our audit objectives.

---

[2] These apprehensions were reported by CBP for fiscal years 2013 through 2015 in the Tucson, Laredo, and Rio Grande Valley Border Patrol sectors.

[3] These seizures of marijuana and cocaine (in pounds) were reported by CBP for fiscal years 2013 through 2015 in the Tucson, Laredo, and Rio Grande Valley Border Patrol sectors.

[4] CBP uses the term "unmanned aircraft systems" for these assets. A UAS is composed of a remotely piloted aircraft, a ground control station, a digital network, and other ground support equipment and personnel required to operate and maintain the system.

CBP HAS MADE PROGRESS IN IMPLEMENTING THE ARIZONA BORDER SURVEILLANCE TECHNOLOGY PLAN, BUT COULD TAKE ADDITIONAL ACTIONS TO STRENGTHEN MANAGEMENT OF THE PLAN

CBP Has Initiated or Completed Deployment of Technologies Under the Plan and Has Taken Actions To Update Program Schedules and Cost Estimates

In March 2014 and April 2015, we reported that CBP had made progress in deploying programs under the Arizona Border Surveillance Technology Plan, but that CBP could take additional action to strengthen its management of the Plan and the Plan's programs.[5] As of May 2016, CBP has initiated or completed deployment of technology to Arizona for each of the programs under the Plan.[6] Additionally, as discussed further below, CBP has reported taking steps to update program schedules and life-cycle cost estimates for the 3 highest-cost programs under the Plan. For example, in May 2016, CBP provided us with complete schedules for 2 of the programs, and we will be reviewing them to determine the extent to which they address our recommendation.

In March 2014, we found that CBP had a schedule for deployment of each of the Plan's 7 programs, and that 4 of the programs would not meet their originally-planned completion dates. We also found that some of the programs had experienced delays relative to their baseline schedules, as of March 2013.[7] Further, in our March 2016 assessment of DHS's major acquisitions programs,[8] we reported on the status of the Plan's Integrated Fixed Tower (IFT) program, noting that from March 2012 to January 2016, the program's initial and full operational capability dates had slipped.[9] Specifically, we reported that the initial operational capability date had slipped from the end of September 2013 to the end of September 2015, and the full operational capability to the end of September 2020. We also reported that this slippage in initial operational capability dates had contributed to slippage in the IFT's full operational capability—primarily as a result of funding shortfalls—and that the IFT program continued to face significant funding shortfalls from fiscal year 2016 to fiscal year 2020.

Despite these delays, as of May 2016 CBP reported that it has initiated or completed deployment of technology to Arizona for each of the 3 highest-cost programs under the plan—IFT, the Remote Video Surveillance System (RVSS), and the Mobile Surveillance Capability (MSC). Specifically, CBP officials stated that MSC deployments in Arizona are complete and that in April 2016, requirements to transition sustainment from the contractor to CBP had been finalized. CBP also reported that the RVSS system has been deployed, and testing on these systems is on-going in 4 out of 5 stations. Further, CBP reported it had initiated deployment of the IFT systems and as of May 2016 has deployed 7 out of 53 IFTs in one area of responsibility. CBP conditionally accepted the system in March 2016 and is working to deploy the remaining IFT unit systems to other areas in the Tucson sector.

With regard to schedules, we previously reported that CBP had at least partially met the 4 characteristics of reliable schedules for the IFT and RVSS schedules and partially or minimally met the 4 characteristics for the MSC schedule. Scheduling best practices are summarized into 4 characteristics of reliable schedules—comprehensive, well-constructed, credible, and controlled (i.e., schedules are periodically

---

[5] GAO, *Arizona Border Surveillance Technology Plan: Additional Actions Needed to Strengthen Management and Assess Effectiveness*, GAO–14–368 (Washington, DC: Mar. 3, 2014), and *Homeland Security Acquisitions: Major Program Assessments Reveal Actions Needed to Improve Accountability*, GAO–15–171SP (Washington, DC: Apr. 22, 2015).

[6] The Plan's 7 acquisition programs include fixed and mobile surveillance systems, agent portable devices, and ground sensors. Its 3 highest-cost programs, which represent 97 percent of the Plan's estimated cost are the Integrated Fixed Tower (IFT), Remote Video Surveillance System (RVSS), and Mobile Surveillance Capability (MSC). The IFT consists of towers with, among other things, ground surveillance radars and surveillance cameras mounted on fixed (that is, stationary) towers. The RVSS includes multiple color and infrared cameras mounted on monopoles, lattice towers, and buildings and differs from the IFT in, among other things, the RVSS does not include radars. The MSC is a stand-alone, truck-mounted suite of radar and cameras that provides a display within the cab of the truck.

[7] The baseline schedule is to represent the original configuration of the program plan and to signify the consensus of all stakeholders regarding the required sequence of events, resource assignments, and acceptable dates for key deliverables. The current schedule is to represent the actual plan to date.

[8] GAO, *Homeland Security Acquisitions: DHS Has Strengthened Management, but Execution and Affordability Concerns Endure*, GAO–16–338SP (Washington, DC: Mar. 31, 2016).

[9] Initial operational capability is defined as the deployment of 7 IFT systems in the area of responsibility for the Nogales Border Patrol station. Full operational capability is defined as deployment of the IFT system in the additional areas of responsibility of the Sonoita, Douglas, Ajo, Casa Grande, and Wellton Border Patrol stations.

updated and progress is monitored).[10] We assessed CBP's schedules as of March 2013 for the 3 highest-cost programs and reported in March 2014 that schedules for 2 of the programs at least partially met each characteristic (i.e., satisfied about half of the criterion), and the schedule for the other program at least minimally met each characteristic (i.e., satisfied a small portion of the criterion).[11] For example, the schedule for the IFT program partially met the characteristic of being credible in that CBP had performed a schedule risk analysis for the program, but the risk analysis did not include the risks most likely to delay the project or how much contingency reserve was needed. For the MSC program, the schedule minimally met the characteristic of being controlled in that it did not have valid baseline dates for activities or milestones by which CBP could track progress. We recommended that CBP ensure that scheduling best practices are applied to the IFT, RVSS, and MSC schedules. DHS concurred with the recommendation and stated that CBP planned to ensure that scheduling best practices would be applied, as outlined in our schedule assessment guide, when updating the 3 programs' schedules. In May 2016, CBP provided us with complete schedules for the IFT and RVSS programs, and we will be reviewing them to determine the extent to which they address our recommendation.

In March 2014, we also found that CBP had not developed an Integrated Master Schedule for the Plan in accordance with best practices. Rather, CBP had used separate schedules for each program to manage implementation of the Plan, as CBP officials stated that the Plan contains individual acquisition programs rather than integrated programs. However, collectively these programs are intended to provide CBP with a combination of surveillance capabilities to be used along the Arizona border with Mexico, and resources are shared among the programs. According to scheduling best practices, an Integrated Master Schedule is a critical management tool for complex systems that involve a number of different projects, such as the Plan, to allow managers to monitor all work activities, how long activities will take, and how the activities are related to one another. We concluded that developing and maintaining an Integrated Master Schedule for the Plan could help provide CBP a comprehensive view of the Plan and help CBP better understand how schedule changes in each individual program could affect implementation of the overall plan.

We recommended that CBP develop an Integrated Master Schedule for the Plan. CBP did not concur with this recommendation and maintained that an Integrated Master Schedule for the Plan in one file undermines the DHS-approved implementation strategy for the individual programs making up the Plan, and that the implementation of this recommendation would essentially create a large, aggregated program, and effectively create an aggregated "system of systems." DHS further stated that a key element of the Plan has been the disaggregation of technology procurements. However, as we noted in the 2014 report, collectively these programs are intended to provide CBP with a combination of surveillance capabilities to be used along the Arizona border with Mexico. Moreover, while the programs themselves may be independent of one another, the Plan's resources are being shared among the programs. We continue to believe that developing an Integrated Master Schedule for the Plan is needed. Developing and maintaining an Integrated Master Schedule for the Plan could allow CBP insight into current or programmed allocation of resources for all programs as opposed to attempting to resolve any resource constraints for each program individually.

In addition, in March 2014, we reported that the life-cycle cost estimates for the Plan reflected some, but not all, best practices. Cost-estimating best practices are summarized into 4 characteristics—well-documented, comprehensive, accurate, and credible. Our analysis of CBP's estimate for the Plan and estimates completed at the time of our review for the 2 highest-cost programs—the IFT and RVSS pro-

---

[10] GAO, *GAO Schedule Assessment Guide: Best Practices for Project Schedules,* GAO–16–89G (Washington, DC: Dec. 2015). We developed this guide through a compilation of best practices that Federal agencies and industry use. According to this guide, for a schedule to be comprehensive, among other things, the schedule should: (1) Capture all activities, as defined in the work breakdown structure; (2) reflect what resources are needed to do the work; and (3) establish the duration of all activities and have specific start and end dates. To be well-constructed, among other things, a schedule should have all of its activities sequenced in the order that they are to be implemented with the most straightforward logic possible. To be credible, the schedule should reflect the order of events necessary to achieve aggregated products or outcomes, and activities in varying levels of the schedule map to one another. Moreover, a schedule risk analysis should be conducted to predict a level of confidence in meeting the program's completion date. For a schedule to be controlled, the schedule should be updated periodically using actual progress and logic to realistically forecast dates for program activities, and a baseline schedule should be maintained to measure, monitor, and report the program's progress.

[11] GAO–14–368.

grams—showed that these estimates at least partially met 3 of these characteristics: Well-documented, comprehensive, and accurate. In terms of being credible, these estimates had not been verified with independent cost estimates in accordance with best practices. We concluded that ensuring that scheduling best practices were applied to the programs' schedules and verifying life-cycle cost estimates with independent estimates could help better ensure the reliability of the schedules and estimates, and we recommended that CBP verify the life-cycle cost estimates for the IFT and RVSS programs with independent cost estimates and reconcile any differences. DHS concurred with this recommendation, but stated then that it did not believe that there would be a benefit in expending funds to obtain independent cost estimates and that if the costs realized to date continued to hold, there may be no requirement or value added in conducting full-blown updates with independent cost estimates.

We recognize the need to balance the cost and time to verify the life-cycle cost estimates with the benefits to be gained from verification with independent cost estimates. CBP officials stated that in fiscal year 2016, DHS's Cost Analysis Division would begin piloting DHS's independent cost estimate capability on the RVSS program. According to CBP officials, this pilot is an opportunity to assist DHS in developing its independent cost estimate capability and that CBP selected the RVSS program for the pilot because the program is at a point in its planning and execution process where it can benefit most from having an independent cost estimate performed as these technologies are being deployed along the Southwest Border, beyond Arizona. CBP officials stated that details for an estimated independent cost estimate schedule and analysis plan for the RVSS program have not been finalized. CBP plans to provide an update on the schedule and analysis plan as additional details become available, and provide information on the final reconciliation of the independent cost estimate and the RVSS program cost estimate once the pilot has been completed at the end of fiscal year 2017. Further, CBP officials have not detailed similar plans for the IFT. We continue to believe that independently verifying the life-cycle cost estimates for the IFT and RVSS programs and reconciling any differences, consistent with best practices, could help CBP better ensure the reliability of the estimates.[12]

CBP Has Made Progress Toward Assessing Performance of Surveillance Technologies, but Has Not Fully Applied Performance Metrics or Assessed the Contributions of Its Technologies

We reported in March 2014 that CBP had identified mission benefits of its surveillance technologies to be deployed under the Plan, such as improved situational awareness and agent safety. However the agency had not developed key attributes for performance metrics for all surveillance technologies to be deployed as part of the Plan, as we recommended in November 2011.[13] Further, in March 2014, we found that CBP did not capture complete data on the contributions of these technologies, which in combination with other relevant performance metrics or indicators, could be used to better determine the impact of CBP's surveillance technologies on CBP's border security efforts, and inform resource allocation decisions. Although CBP had a field within its Enforcement Integrated Database for data on whether technological assets, such as SBInet surveillance towers, and nontechnological assets, such as canine teams, assisted or contributed to the apprehension of illegal entrants and seizure of drugs and other contraband, according to CBP officials, Border Patrol Agents were not required to record these data. This limited CBP's ability to collect, track, and analyze available data on asset assists to help monitor the contribution of surveillance technologies, including its SBInet system, to Border Patrol apprehensions and seizures and inform resource allocation decisions. We recommended that CBP require data on asset assists to be recorded and tracked within its database, and once these data were required to be recorded and tracked, that it analyze available data on apprehensions and technological assists—in combination with other relevant performance metrics or indicators, as appropriate—to determine the contribution of surveillance technologies to CBP's border security efforts. CBP concurred with our recommendations and has implemented one of them. Specifically, in June 2014, CBP issued guidance informing Border Patrol Agents that the asset assist data field within its database was now a mandatory data field.

---

[12] GAO, *2015 Annual Report: Additional Opportunities to Reduce Fragmentation, Overlap, and Duplication and Achieve Other Financial Benefits*, GAO–15–404SP (Washington, DC: Apr. 14, 2015).

[13] See GAO–14–368, and *Arizona Border Surveillance Technology: More Information on Plans and Costs Is Needed before Proceeding*, GAO–12–22 (Washington, DC: Nov. 4, 2011).

Agents are required to enter any assisting surveillance technology or other equipment before proceeding.

Further, as of May 2015, CBP had identified a set of potential key attributes for performance metrics for all technologies to be deployed under the Plan. However, CBP officials stated that this set of performance metrics was under review as the agency continued to refine the key attributes for metrics to assess the contributions and impacts of surveillance technology on its border security mission.[14] In our March 2016 update on the progress made by agencies to address our findings on duplication and cost savings across the Federal Government, we reported that CBP had modified its time frame for developing baselines for each performance measure and that additional time would be needed to implement and apply key attributes for metrics. According to CBP officials, CBP expected these performance measure baselines to be developed by the end of calendar year 2015, at which time the agency planned to begin using the data to evaluate the individual and collective contributions of specific technology assets deployed under the Plan. Moreover, CBP planned to use the baseline data to establish a tool that explains the qualitative and quantitative impacts of technology and tactical infrastructure on situational awareness in specific areas of the border environment by the end of fiscal year 2016. While CBP had expected to complete its development of baselines for each performance measure by the end of calendar year 2015, as of March 2016 the actual completion is being adjusted pending test and evaluation results for recently deployed technologies on the Southwest Border. Until CBP completes its efforts to fully develop and apply key attributes for performance metrics for all technologies to be deployed under the Plan, it will not be well-positioned to fully assess its progress in implementing the Plan and determining when mission benefits have been fully realized.

CBP UTILIZES UNMANNED PREDATOR B AIRCRAFT AND TACTICAL AEROSTATS FOR A VARIETY OF BORDER SECURITY ACTIVITIES

Preliminary Observations on CBP's Utilization of Predator B Aircraft

Our on-going work shows that as of May 2016, CBP operates 9 Predator B from 4 AMO National Air Security Operations Centers (NASOC) located in Sierra Vista, Arizona; Grand Forks, North Dakota; Corpus Christi, Texas; and Jacksonville, Florida.[15] Three Predator B aircraft are assigned to the NASOCs in Arizona, North Dakota, and Texas while the NASOC in Florida remotely operates Predator B aircraft launched from the other NASOCs. AMO began operation of Predator B aircraft in fiscal year 2006, and all 4 NASOCs became operational in fiscal year 2011. See figure 1 for a photograph of a CBP Predator B aircraft.

---

[14] GAO-15-404SP.

[15] AMO's NASOCs perform specialized missions Nation-wide and in the Caribbean, eastern Pacific, and Central America, using Predator B, long-range patrol aircraft, and other aircraft. From 2010 to 2013, AMO operated a NASOC in Cape Canaveral, Florida, for UAS operations.

Source: CBP. | GAO-16-671T

CBP's Predator B aircraft may be equipped with video and radar sensors utilized primarily to support the operations of other CBP components, and Federal, State, and local law enforcement agencies.[16] CBP's Predator B operations in support of its components and other law enforcement agencies include patrol missions to detect the illegal entry of goods and people at and between U.S. POEs and investigative missions to provide aerial support for law enforcement activities and investigations. For example, CBP's Predator B video and radar sensors support Border Patrol activities to identify and apprehend individuals entering the United States between POEs. CBP collects and tracks information on the number of assists provided for apprehensions of individuals and seizures of contraband, including narcotics, in support of law enforcement operations by Predator B aircraft. In addition, CBP's Predator B aircraft have been deployed to provide aerial support for monitoring natural disasters such as wildfires and floods. For example, CBP's Predator B were deployed in 2010 and 2011 to support Federal, State, and local Government agencies in response to flooding in the Red River Valley area of North Dakota.

CBP's Predator B aircraft operate in the U.S. National airspace system in accordance with Federal Aviation Administration (FAA) requirements for authorizing all UAS operations in the National Airspace System.[17] In accordance with FAA requirements, all Predator B flights must comply with a Certificate of Waiver or Authorization (COA). The COA-designated airspace establishes operational corridors for Predator B activity both along and within 100 miles of the border for the Northern Border, and along and within 25 to 60 miles of the border for the Southern Border, exclusive of urban areas. COAs issued by FAA to CBP also include airspace for training missions which involve take-offs and landings around a designated NASOC and transit missions to move Predator B aircraft between NASOCs. As of May 2016,

---

[16] Predator B sensors include: Electro-optical and infrared camera that collects full-motion video, Vehicle and Dismount Exploitation Radar (VADER) which collects radar images of moving objects, synthetic-aperture radar that collects radar images that show terrain and structures and allow for analysis to detect change over time, and SeaVue radar which collects radar images of maritime vessels.

[17] See Federal Aviation Administration, Notice N JO 7210.889: Unmanned Aircraft Operations in the National Airspace System (Oct. 27, 2015). The National Airspace System is the network of United States airspace that includes the interconnected and interdependent network of systems, procedures, facilities, aircraft, and people.

CBP has utilized the NASOC in North Dakota as a location to train new and existing CBP Predator B pilots. For our on-going work, we analyzed CBP data on reported Predator B COA-designated flight hours from fiscal years 2011 to 2015 and found that 81 percent of flight hours were associated with COA-designated airspace along border and coastal areas. For more information on Predator B flight hours in COA-designated airspace, see figure 2.

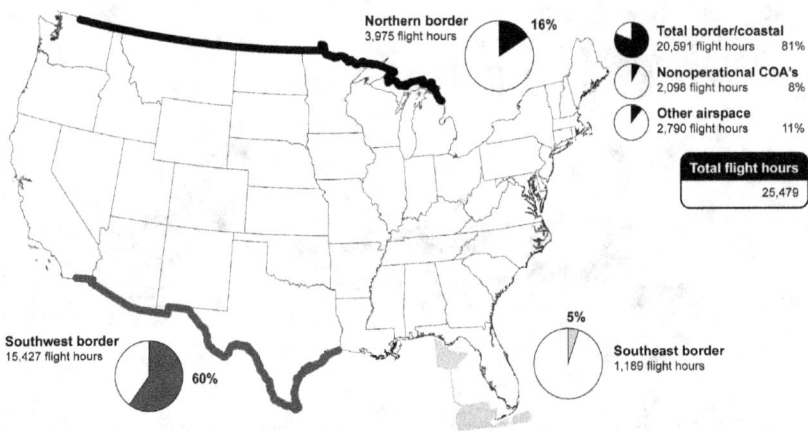

Based on our on-going work, we found that airspace access and weather can impact CBP's ability to utilize Predator B aircraft. According to CBP officials we spoke with in Arizona, Predator B flights may be excluded from restricted airspace managed by the Department of Defense along border areas which can affect the ability of Predator B to support Border Patrol. CBP officials we spoke with in Arizona and Texas told us that Predator B missions are affected by hazardous weather conditions that can affect their ability to operate the aircraft. According to CBP officials we spoke with in Texas, CBP took steps to mitigate the impact of hazardous weather in January and February 2016 by deploying one Predator B aircraft from Corpus Christi, Texas, to San Angelo, Texas, at San Angelo Regional Airport which had favorable weather conditions. CBP's deployment of a Predator B at San Angelo Regional Airport was in accordance with a FAA-issued COA to conduct its border security mission in Texas and lasted approximately 3 weeks. We plan to evaluate how these factors affect CBP's utilization of Predator B aircraft as part of our on-going work.

Preliminary Observations on CBP's Utilization of Tactical Aerostats in South Texas

Our on-going work shows that as of May 2016, CBP has deployed 6 tactical aerostats along the U.S.-Mexico border in south Texas to support Border Patrol. Specifically, CBP deployed 5 tactical aerostats in Border Patrol's Rio Grande Valley sector and 1 tactical aerostat In Laredo sector. CBP utilizes 3 types of tactical aerostats equipped with cameras for capturing full-motion video: Persistent Threat Detection System (PTDS), Persistent Ground Surveillance System (PGSS), and Rapid Aerostat Initial Deployment (RAID). Each type of tactical aerostat varies in size and altitude of operation. See figure 3 for a photograph of a RAID aerostat. CBP owns the RAID aerostats and leases PTDS and PGSS aerostats through the Department of Defense. CBP operates its tactical aerostats in accordance with FAA regulations through the issuance of a COA.[18]

---

[18] See 14 C.F.R. pt. 101. These rules govern operation in the United States of, among other things, any balloon that is moored to the surface of the earth or an object thereon and that has a diameter of more than 6 feet or a gas capacity of more than 115 cubic feet. Id. at § 101.1(a)(1).

Source: GAO. | GAO-16-671T

Tactical aerostats were first deployed and evaluated by CBP in August 2012 in south Texas. CBP's Office of Technology Innovation and Acquisition manages aerostat technology and the operation of each site through contracts, while Border Patrol Agents operate tactical aerostat cameras and provide security at each site. As of May 2016, Border Patrol has taken actions to track the contribution of tactical aerostats to its mission activities. Specifically, agents track and record the number of assists aerostats provide for apprehensions of individuals and seizures of contraband and narcotics.

Based on our on-going work, we found that airspace access, weather, and real estate can impact CBP's ability to deploy and utilize tactical aerostats in south Texas.
- *Airspace access.*—Aerostat site placement is subject to FAA approval to ensure the aerostat does not converge on dedicated flight paths.
- *Weather.*—Aerostat flight is subject to weather restrictions, such as hazardous weather involving high winds or storms.
- *Real estate.*—Aerostat sites utilized by CBP involve access to private property and land owner acceptance, and right of entry is required prior for placement. In addition, CBP must take into consideration any relevant environmental and wildlife impacts prior to deployment of a tactical aerostat, such as flood zones, endangered species, migratory animals, among others.

We plan to evaluate how these factors affect CBP's utilization of tactical aerostats as part of our on-going work.

Chairwoman McSally, Ranking Member Vela, and Members of the subcommittee, this concludes my prepared statement. I will be happy to answer any questions you may have.

Ms. MCSALLY. Thanks, Ms. Gambler.

I now recognize myself for 5 minutes for questions.

I want to start off with Ms. Gambler. Are you familiar with our Border Security Technology Accountability Act?

Ms. GAMBLER. I am, yes, Chairwoman.

Ms. MCSALLY. Can you share, from your perspective and your expertise, and whether that is going to assist in any of the challenges that you have raised in the past and continue to be issues?

Ms. GAMBLER. Absolutely. That bill is very consistent with the findings and messages from GAO's prior work looking at CBP's efforts to deploy surveillance technologies. For example, the bill calls for making sure that technologies have acquisition program baselines in place, that the programs are monitored according to cost schedule and performance, and those address a number of the key findings that we have had related to CBP's technology programs. I might also add that it is reflective of leading practices and best practices for acquisition management.

Ms. McSALLY. Great. Thank you.

I just want to say, again, this has unanimously passed in the House. It is being held up in the Senate. It was reported out of committee. I mean, we are hearing, you know, rumors that it is being held up because our colleagues don't want us to have a win on any border security issue. I hope from, just your comments today and looking at the bill, that they would realize that this is a win for the taxpayers; this is a win for our improvement and processes for it being able to secure our border, and I hope we can get past the partisan bickering, and actually move this thing forward so we can put it into force.

Okay. Next question I want to ask, really, Chief Vitiello, General Alles, Mr. Borkowski. As I opened up, I mentioned, I think, some of the initiatives you are doing are increasing a good common operational picture and providing good information that might be good for intelligence assessment to understand, kind-of, you know, where the cartels are operating. But if we are not getting it into the agent's hand, if they are not getting the information that the people back in the operation center have, then, you know, we still have more steps to make, right? So that they can, not have information overload, but actually have the best situation awareness possible.

So of the technologies mentioned, or maybe some that are under development, which ones are actually in the hands of the agents that are out there intercepting the activity, or are they getting information over a radio? I want to—I just want to have a sense of, like, where they are in getting that information and what other initiatives might be in the pipeline in order to improve situation awareness for the agents that are out there?

Mr. VITIELLO. Thanks for that question.

A lot of what the agents, and what we have invested in, and what we have been able to take from the DOD reuse, are association with the Department of Defense to take some of their excess material and equipment and put that in the hands of agents. So, obviously, the things that they use, the terminal binoculars, the long-range assistance to their vision, those are all hand-held. Some of those are truck-mounted, so those are all in the hands of the agents. So the agents that are operating that equipment can, in real time, inform response teams that are deployed with them in close proximity, the towers, the cameras, the RVSS. There is a combination of some of that being deployed at the sector level. So there is a command center in Tucson where the sector is, and that activity is then dispatched for response in that location.

Ms. McSALLY. But is that by voice? That is what I am trying to get at. You might have a ground sensor; you have got a predator flying; you have got the information from the IFTs. We have perfect situational awareness in the command center. Again, I have been there in the military, where you understate exactly where the traffic is, but then you are telling the poor guy, poor gal on the run on a radio, like, here is what is happening. Are there tools that is actually getting that situation awareness to the agent that is not just a voice call?

Mr. VITIELLO. Yes. So it is via voice, but there are precise measurements being taken by the hits that the sensors get on the aircraft. Our own towers, our own sensors are deployed. All of that material and those sensors are geo-referenced, and the agents are getting precise details about where that activity is occurring, and then the classification, you know, what kind of threat do they face, how big are the groups, et cetera, that does go over voice to them. But they are deployed in that same proximity as well.

So there is a balance that has to be struck in terms of how much goes over the air and how much they get in their—in their hands as far as using tablets and all those kinds of things. We are doing some experiments about getting the information closer to them as it is occurring. There is also an information stream that they need to be aware of. Right? So when the classification comes through, that they prioritize the threat information versus just activity writ large.

Ms. MCSALLY. Great.

Is there anything, Mr. Borkowski, in the works? Again, when I was flying my A–10, I am actually talking to guys on the ground that are seeing what I am seeing, my targeting pod, so their situational awareness increased.

Mr. BORKOWSKI. We are clearly, as you suggest, getting kind-of, demand for, give me blue force tracking, give me the picture that the camera is showing. We don't have that today. There are a couple of reasons. One is we don't have the infrastructure to send it. So that is one of the things we are struggling with.

Having said that, both with DHS and with DOD, which has some of these technologies, our agents have been exposed and are piloting those things. I still have to figure out how to get the pipe, you know, to send it. But we are creating a demand from that. We are looking at technologies that DOD has. We have a project with DHS and border security awareness, which will look at this question. We have to handle the pipeline.

One other thing I would add is, one of the things that broke badly on SBInet was there was a tremendous investment in this particular question that was not tightly defined. We actually had to pull away from that in order to build the hardware. Now that we have the hardware, we believe we are starting to get a tighter definition. But you are right. We need to crack that. There are a couple things that are really in the way. The biggest one that bothers me is the bandwidth to get the signal across.

Ms. MCSALLY. Yes. Okay. Thank you.

All right, we are going to do a couple of rounds here, but I wanted to give opportunity for others, including the Ranking Member of the full committee.

Mr. THOMPSON. Thank you, Madam Chair, and thank you, Ranking Member.

Some of us have been around a little while, and we have seen procurements come and go. I guess I will ask Ms. Gambler: Your review of the systems, can you share with the committee your analysis of whether or not we are getting better at procurements? Or we are about where we have been all the time?

Ms. GAMBLER. I think in this area, as it relates to border security, I think there has been some progress made, even relative to what we reported on 2 years ago as it relates to technologies under the Arizona Surveillance Technology Plan.

CBP has been updating their schedules for some of the programs. They—what is called rebaselined the IFT program late last year. They are working on piloting an independent cost estimate for the RVSS program. So I think in certain areas, Ranking Member Thompson, they have made progress. I think there are still some key areas where we would like to see some additional progress, including for them to be able to assess what they are getting out of the systems. We are also, as we are starting some new work in these areas interested to see the results of some of the testing that's been done on the systems that has been recently deployed. So that is still, I think, an open question for us.

Mr. THOMPSON. Thank you. I would—Mr. Borkowski, were you around with SBInet?

Mr. BORKOWSKI. Yes. I was brought in to try to clean up SBInet, but yes, I was around for——

Mr. THOMPSON. So you know where I am going, right?

Mr. BORKOWSKI. I have a suspicion, sir.

Mr. THOMPSON. Can you tell me if your clean-up has been complete? Can you give the committee assurance that the missteps made with SBInet won't be made again?

Mr. BORKOWSKI. Well, I could never assure you that we would never make another misstep. I can tell you that the odds of such a misstep are much lower, the risk of such a misstep is much lower than it was.

We learned a lot from SBInet, and you know, we accommodated as much of that lesson as we could into this process. Having said that, we are still in the process of training people to be skilled acquisition program managers. They are getting better, but we are still in the process of training people.

We are still——

Mr. THOMPSON. How much of a reliance—excuse me. Are we relying on outside contractors to do that? Have we been able to pull that capacity within the organization?

Mr. BORKOWSKI. We do have contractors supporting us, but we have built organic, you know, Government employee skills that probably did not exist 4 years ago.

So we do have program managers who are skilled. I wish I had more of them. I think that is part of the challenge is having enough people to meet all of the demands. So we have a mix of contractors, but in the past, we were much more reliant on those contractors to augment our own lack of skills. We have spent a great deal of time, both in CBP and in DHS in building up the Government employee workforce skills.

Mr. THOMPSON. So is building up the Government workforce capacity an issue of you not being able to find the people, or you don't have the money if you found them, to employ them?

Mr. BORKOWSKI. I think it is both. But there are people out there. The money is a challenge. We compete, obviously, for Border

Patrol Agents, CBP Officers, and frankly, if you had to ask what the priority is, I think it is Border Patrol Agents and CBP Officers. So we compete. We come after that, as I think we should. Money is an issue. There is also the hiring process is very long for a whole variety of reasons.

So when we do identify people, sometimes it is very difficult for them to wait out the hiring process. So there are those kinds of issues as well.

Mr. THOMPSON. So how long does it take to hire somebody?

Mr. BORKOWSKI. It can take a year-plus in some cases, depending on where—you know, how many people are in the queue. We are talking about Border Patrol Agents, CBP Officers, our own mission support people. We have background investigations. There are a whole bunch of people who are competing for the resources to do background investigations, so it could be months, and go to a year.

Mr. THOMPSON. Have you highlighted your lack of being able to get people in a reasonable period of time as one of the weaknesses in the operation?

Mr. BORKOWSKI. I think as CBP corporately has spent a great deal of time on that question and issue about being able to hire people. Yes, sir.

Mr. THOMPSON. Madam Chair, I think at some point, we might order from a human resources standpoint look at it, because all of us running the people all the time who are very qualified, who want to work for the Government——

Mr. BORKOWSKI. Yes.

Mr. THOMPSON [continuing]. But if you tell them it takes a year, something like that, we ought to be able to come up with a better way of vetting people and getting them into the system.

Mr. BORKOWSKI. I agree.

Mr. THOMPSON. I guess the last point is, it costs more to have outside contractors, right?

Mr. BORKOWSKI. Not always, sir. It is actually a case-by-case, so not always. But I believe it is—if I had my druthers, I would have kind of a 2–1 ratio, Government-to-outside contractors, and right now I am about 50–50. There are some skills that are very difficult to get, frankly, at Government salaries, but it depends. It is not always cheaper to have Government than contractors. It depends on case-by-case.

Mr. THOMPSON. So you wanted two-thirds or one-third?

Mr. BORKOWSKI. My sense is that would be about ideal. The reason for that is I want the capacity to, first of all have, surge, right? Government employees are good, steady state. I want to be able to surge, and contractor employees are very good for that.

The other reason that I think contractors sometimes help is there are some very kind of scarce highly technical skills that are more accessible through contractors in many cases than through Government employees.

Mr. THOMPSON. Thank you, Madam Chair.

Ms. MCSALLY. Thanks. I want to thank the Ranking Member of the full committee.

In our last hearing here in the District of Columbia, we highlighted some of these manning issues for the CBP Officers at the port of entry. It took about 18 months. The Border Jobs for Veterans Act, which we passed, such as my bill, supposed to fast-track our veterans. The goal would be 90 days, but there is still a lot of work to do and lot of concerns and challenges. But, really, everybody on the subcommittee and across the committee that we have heard, so I think we still have a lot of work to do.

Mr. THOMPSON. Right. I am just trying to make sure that we don't lose sight of the fact that that process is still—and what have you, and I would like my full statement to be admitted into the record.

Ms. MCSALLY. Without objection. Thank you, Ranking Member.

Ms. MCSALLY. The Chair now recognizes the Ranking Member of the subcommittee, Mr. Vela.

Mr. VELA. So General Alles, what can you tell us about the issues in Corpus Christi with the predator being the weather?

Mr. ALLES. So for Corpus Christi, sir, that actually, for the predator overall, weather is a challenge for the system.

Generally, it runs about a 20 percent higher cancellation rate than our manned aircraft for weather. So one of the efforts we are making currently, system-wide, is we are working with General Thomas on our automatic take-off and landing system which will improve the cross limitation of the aircraft. That is one. Then, second, we are looking at working out of divert fields, for instance, we used San Angelo this last year that are better winter weather operating locations. We have also deployed the asset to the transit zone during the wintertime. We get more effective operation out of the platform. We have two platforms right now in Columbia and Barranquilla operating. So that is how we look at the challenges there in Corpus Christi. We get efficiencies out of the site. It is a P–3 site also, so the P–3 pilots not only fly the P–3, but they fly the predator UAS at the same time. That is a great efficiency force in terms of operations, and if we split those sites up, we lose that efficiency. So that is how we tackled it so far, sir.

Mr. VELA. So is the fog the issue basically, or——

Mr. ALLES. Generally, it is ceilings. In the wintertime I went through flight school actually in Kingsville, and I remember on many days sitting there playing AC/DC in the waiting room while the fog and whatever it was hung over. So getting out of that kind of coastal interference zone, I think is advantageous. San Angelo has been a good location.

Our challenge, honestly, has been the FAA there. We have worked through those issues with them. They are very adverse to us operating out of civilian airfields. That is the first time an unmanned aircraft has operated out of a civilian airfield. That has worked well.

Mr. VELA. Now, with respect to these tactical aerostats, how are you dealing with the landowners?

Mr. VITIELLO. So all of the sites need preparatory work, a little bit of what my colleague, Mr. Borkowski, said as it relates to our towers, real estate acquisition and permission to enter lands, et cetera. So all of the sites that are operating now are within—in conjunction with the landowners. Sometimes that is via a lease, sometimes that is a different kind of agreement. But it is all structured and scheduled so that they are aware of our presence. So far, we haven't had any challenges. It was difficult to move a couple of ones that were up north. There was a couple operational decisions, we wanted to move the ones closer to the border because of their effect, and the efficiency that the agents were getting, but all is going well so far.

Mr. VELA. So, Chief, I think you are well aware of the challenges that we have on the other side of the border in Tamaulipas, Mexico with respect to cartel activity, kidnappings, and murders that have, you know, the State's deteriorated, over, you know, the last several years. What I am curious about, is there anything that we can do from your standpoint, technologically, to help in that area?

Mr. VITIELLO. It is a difficult challenge. We feel bad for the people who are a part of those communities. It is such—it is unfortunate that they face that situation. I think as it relates to help from here is to strengthen our relationship and provide Mexico with the mentorship, sharing of best practices, mechanisms to exchange information quickly, and then support their efforts to reform their domestic and their Federal law enforcement.

Mr. VELA. So following up on that, what kind of shared practices are you currently using with law enforcement in Mexico?

Mr. VITIELLO. In its best form, we have programs underway under the border violence prevention protocols. It is a systematic way for us to sit down and understand where the violence is taking place, what it means to our deployments at the border, between the ports and at the ports as well, and then sharing information where it is critical and then it is—in a deployment form, we do joint patrols with authorities in Mexico, in places where we know that violence or smuggling is occurring. It is a great benefit for them to have us close by on our side and then doing the same in Mexico. Those have worked out very well when they have the resources available to do it.

Mr. VELA. Well, thank you.

Before I yield, I would just add that I agree with, Madam Chair, with your perspective on the use of veterans. I think we need to have a much more robust approach around the country with respect to educating our veterans about the availability of these jobs. I think it is something that I surely look forward to working with you on.

Ms. MCSALLY. I agree with the Ranking Member. As long as it doesn't take 18 months for them to get a job. If we can get to that in less than 90 days and while they are still on active duty, that would be ideal. We have to keep working on that bill being implemented for the intent that it was supposed to be. So I appreciate it.

The Chair now recognizes Mr. Rogers from Alabama.

Mr. ROGERS. Thank you, Madam Chairwoman.

I want to revisit this issue of the aerostats. Can you tell me how many aerostats you have in—that are deployed at present?

Mr. VITIELLO. We have 6 deployed in the South Texas area.

Mr. ROGERS. Are they the same model or version or do they differ?

Mr. VITIELLO. There are 2 separate versions, they are both what we call the tactical version. They are both supported by mobile towers that also work the border environment that give us cameras and——

Mr. ROGERS. What do you mean supported by mobile towers? I see the tower on the truck here. Does that have to go somewhere closer to the aerostats?

Mr. VITIELLO. The aerostats, it is a deployment package. They come with towers that could be put up remotely. So when the envelope is flying, when the balloon is up in the air, it has sensors hanging off of it, the EOIR and day cameras, high-definition cameras, and then there are towers that support in the area as well that can monitor the border for us that——

Mr. ROGERS. They receive signals from the aerostat?

Mr. VITIELLO. The signals go to a small command post, and then the information that is obtained there is then dispatched to response units in the field.

Mr. ROGERS. So it doesn't go to the truck that is carrying the tower?

Mr. VITIELLO. So there are other vehicles that we have that are Government equipment that are not DOD reuse; the MVSS, the MSS, which are—have similar equipment on masks in the back of mobile vehicles. Those are operated by Border Patrol Agents, who can then obtain the information from the screens and then distribute it via radio to response teams as well.

Mr. ROGERS. Are all 6 of the aerostats deployed at present?

Mr. VITIELLO. They are.

Mr. ROGERS. How long do they stay up?

Mr. VITIELLO. There is maintenance that is required, recurring maintenance that is required. We are constantly evaluating the readiness rate. They have to be brought down to change envelopes when something happens, when the wind is too high, things like that. But, generally, I think we talked about the other day, they are in the neighborhood of 80 percent up time, so while they are available. They are available 80 percent of the time that they are deployed. But there are conditions which cause us to either do maintenance or bring them down for weather events, et cetera.

Mr. ROGERS. Are you keeping these in a particular sector?

Mr. VITIELLO. Right now they are deployed in South Texas, in what we call the Rio Grande Valley sector, which is the McAllen Rio Grande City area. They are there because as my colleague, Mr. Borkowski, said because we have a planned deployment there for integrated fixed towers for RVSS, for planned mobile trucks, et cetera. That stuff has to catch up our work on the ground to get those sites ready to purchase land, to do the environmental work is underway. In the mean time, we have deployed the aerostats to fill that gap given the activity levels that are in that part of the border.

Mr. ROGERS. Are all 6 of these from the DOD?

Mr. VITIELLO. They are all DOD reuse equipment that we have gotten from them.

Mr. ROGERS. Are there any remaining DOD aerostats available that you have not accepted?

Mr. VITIELLO. I believe they have more, but I am not aware of any that they have that we are actually asking for. I think we have 2 that we are getting ready to deploy elsewhere.

Mr. BORKOWSKI. Sir, there are—there are 3—3 incarnations of this, 2 large ones. DOD owns them, has not accessed them, but basically leases them to us. The smaller ones, which are called Raid. We own, I think, 8 of them. Two of them are deployed, so we have additional ones in storage. We also have towers that we can deploy independently of the Raid. So there are additional aerostats available that we have in storage. They cost, in like $3 million a year to run, so we are pretty judicious in how we apply them and where we apply them, but we do have smaller ones.

Mr. ROGERS. Do you have a need for more than the 6?

Mr. VITIELLO. We prefer to deploy the mobile technology that is on its way to us.

Mr. ROGERS. Why?

Mr. VITIELLO. Excuse me?

Mr. ROGERS. Why?

Mr. VITIELLO. The aerostats are a good gap filler. We see them as a temporary asset. We may not continue to use them in south Texas as the technology plan, the fuller requirement gets deployed. We will take them and use them in a place where the technology has to catch up. So they are a good gap filler. But because of the expense of their operation, operations and maintenance is quite high, so we are looking forward to a time where we have a more permanent infrastructure that is not dependent on the kinds of costs that these bring to us.

Mr. ROGERS. All of these are tethered, correct?

Mr. VITIELLO. They are.

Mr. ROGERS. At what altitude?

Mr. VITIELLO. I believe there is one that is at 1,800 feet, and the other one is something less than that, 12——

Mr. BORKOWSKI. The smaller ones are around 1,000 feet.

Mr. ROGERS. Have you all considered using some of the non-tethered aerostats, then they can loiter for a longer periods of time?

Mr. BORKOWSKI. Like essentially blimps?

Mr. ROGERS. Correct. The Marines use those?

Mr. BORKOWSKI. We have looked at that. Right now, and the problem is we probably have to buy those. Those haven't been assessed. The advantage of these tethered aerostats, is that although we have to pay the operation and maintenance, we didn't actually have to buy the aerostat; we didn't have to buy the tower; we didn't have to buy the camera. That is why these were so attractive to us, and they seem to be the sensible thing for the time being.

Mr. ROGERS. One of the reasons I am so focused on these, is in my trips to the Southwest Border, we have had just a world of trouble with cameras, whether cameras on poles or trucks or whatever. To my knowledge, those problems still exist. Also, I like the fact that they are up high, and you can see further across the border where there is people gathering.

So I am just curious, and this would be my final question, I know my time has expired: What is the downside?

Mr. BORKOWSKI. There are two. One is the cost. We are trying to drive those costs down. But it is $3 million or more for the bigger ones a year for these things.

The second thing is that they are very weather-dependent. The Chief talked about 80 percent, but there are times of the year where we can have availability down to 60 percent depending on the weather. So you really have to kind-of have to trade their availability for the mission and their cost. So our sense is that there are probably areas where aerostats will make sense, but they are probably not the right long-term solution. We are using them like very high towers, as you suggested. And there are areas where they see over foliage, but in the areas where we are using them, we actually think the lower cost, more permanent, more highly-available fixed infrastructure makes more sense for the long term. We are still studying where the aerostats might have a long-term future, but it will probably be in spots.

Mr. ROGERS. I won't ask any more questions, but I would, Madam Chairwoman, like to, at some point, revisit the idea of micro sats to see if they are using any of those.

With that, I yield back.

Ms. MCSALLY. The gentleman yields.

The Chair now recognizes Ms. Torres of California for questions for 5 minutes.

Mrs. TORRES. Thank you, Chairwoman.

How is CBP measuring the effectiveness of the technology deployed at the border, and what matrix are used and how does that compare over time?

Mr. VITIELLO. So we are collecting all—several elements of what you might call output measures, the number of arrests that have been made, how often in a particular area, agency assaults, the kinds of seizures that are being made, and we look at that in conjunction with the kinds of deployments that exist in those areas. As our colleague from the GAO reported, we are looking at systems that allow us at the time of arrest, as we are recording activity, to then attribute the—when there is a seizure or an arrest made, attribute the assist of the technology in those areas. Over time, you can start to look at the effect of certain kinds of deployments and how they contribute to seizures and arrests. That way, we can see which are the most valuable kinds of assets and how they are deployed or whether we need to make changes to those deployments.

Mrs. TORRES. So over time, is this technology going to be able to utilize over actual manpower?

Mr. VITIELLO. So we—our experience is, is that when we deploy in an area with the technology, be it mobile or fixed, we start to see more activity, because we turn the information—the information is more available. You know more about an area once these deployments occur. So there is usually more activity in the beginnings of those deployments.

But over time, smuggling patterns change. The activity changes, the arrest and the effectiveness of the deployments of the agents themselves and the responses start to change that activity, and the smugglers look for other locations to enter in. So we have seen that sort of a spike in activity in the immediate aftermath of a robust deployment, and then we see the traffic shift and move, and then we—that is why it is important to have these gap fillers, that is why it is important to have mobile technology so we can be assured to be in the right place at the right time.

Mrs. TORRES. I understand that they are—there is a need to make a serious commitment, financial commitment, and it is going to be a lot more—it is a lot more costlier in the beginning, but over time, you know, my question really is, is it smart to spend this much money upfront? Are we going to save it in having actual personnel costs, you know, a few years down the road, and how long? Are we really looking at that, at those statistics?

Mr. VITIELLO. When you look at where we have gotten to on how we decided on the deployment, the Arizona Technology Plan is one, our plans for the other border deployments, we looked at—and Mark can speak more precisely about the analysis of alternatives—we looked at which technologies would be most advantageous. We used our experience and the feedback from users to decide in the CGAP process what technologies to use.

But you are going to have to have—it is our opinion and our experience that you are going to have to have a mix. It might be more expensive on the front end to install the technology, but over time you see benefits of that. Sometimes that is fewer deployments in particular areas so that we can use the workforce more efficiently.

Mrs. TORRES. Yeah. Over time, I can see where you can modify equipment a lot easier than personnel habits.

How is CBP defining situational awareness and operational control?

Mr. VITIELLO. So, on the situational awareness side, we are looking at the border in a couple of different ways. Situational awareness, as defined, is us being able to understand what is happening, have a predictive analysis, like, know where particular areas of the border are going to be problematic or where we know we are going to have traffic, and then have the kind of assets that are available, technology and the resources, agents on the line, in those locations to give ourselves real-time information about what is going on in that area.

Mrs. TORRES. Are all of these metrics that you are utilizing public, made public, this information?

Mr. VITIELLO. So, on the CBP site, the CBP.gov, there are output statistics about the kinds of activities, arrests. Those are usually posted at the end of each month, and so people can see that there.

Mrs. TORRES. So this is where the public can better understand whether these investments are actually paying out in ensuring, you know, that we are minimizing the number of crossings?

Mr. VITIELLO. So the statistics that are typically on the site don't attribute the work to the technology. It is more sort of an output measure of what is happening month by month.

Mrs. TORRES. Okay.

Thank you.

Ms. MCSALLY. All right. Great. I am going to continue on with another round here. I have a lot of questions now that I have you all here.

So I want to follow up, the Arizona Technology Plan, when fully complete—well, let me start with this, actually, Chief Vitiello. Our first hearing I had when I took over, you stated that, of the 2,000 miles of the border, you have situational awareness of about 56 percent of that border, Southern Border, right now.

So for the Arizona Technology Plan, what percentage of that, of the miles of the Arizona border, did we have situational awareness of? Then, when complete, when it is fully rolled out, are we going to have 100 percent situational awareness so if it moves we see it, when the whole plan is implemented?

Mr. VITIELLO. Yeah, so last time I was here I might not have been as precise as I wanted to be as it relates to situational awareness.

The 56 percent measure, at that time—and this changes quarter by quarter—was the areas of the border where the deployment itself advises the workforce, advises the response agents, advises us of what is happening in real time. So, at that time, about 56 percent of the border had a deployment that was responsive enough to know in real time when activity occurred at the border.

So a response in real time—within, you know, a shift, agents knew about an entry and were able to mount a response.

Ms. MCSALLY. Okay. So I think maybe that is a definition issue. To me, that is operational control. Situational awareness is, if you see it—I mean, if it moves, you see it. That is, like, you know, metric No. 1. The second metric is, when you see it, you can get to it and stop it. That is the operational control piece, right?

So we were just trying to get a sense of, of the 2,000 miles of the border, if it moves and it is coming across the border, it is trying to breach, you actually see it. You may not be able to get to it, but you at least see it. So is there a different number that is not 56 percent?

Mr. VITIELLO. What we are trying do in this state of the border reporting that we are putting in our system and using for things like CGAP and using to inform our deployments, there is a level of situational awareness across the entire border. So the 56 percent number, that is happening in real time; the sensors, the agents themselves, the deployments are picking up that activity in real time and being able to respond to it.

The rest of the border, we are using other technology to monitor it regularly, but there is not an immediate response in each of those cases. That other part of the border, where we are using GEOINT, where we are using change detection to monitor the border, it is not solely that. We have other methods of being able to monitor what is going on in those areas. But there is not necessarily a deployment or a sensor that picks up that activity. It is more of this change detection, using the UAS, using other assets to monitor the border.

But I would say that, as it relates to situational awareness, how we see it, each and every zone of the border has some level of monitoring that occurs in it, whether it be our assets directly deployed, whether it be the community informing us of things that are going on or our own assets that are doing a monitoring that verify to us that there is or isn't activity going on.

Ms. MCSALLY. Okay. Yeah, I think we just have different definitions of situational awareness. I mean, I appreciate that some of the VADER stuff and change detection you are doing is, after the fact, being able to look back and kind of see some of the changes that have happened, which is really important for intelligence and, you know, predictive analysis and all that.

Again, I am just a fighter pilot, and I am just trying to get down to, like, a simple metric of, if it is breaching, if it is about to cross the border, we see it in real time. In 2,000 miles of the border, where do we have—we may not be able to get to it, we may lose it, but we see it happening real time.

So, I mean, I don't want to waste a lot of time going back and forth on this, but I think that is one of the frustrations, I would say, of this committee and definitely of my constituents, is we don't know what the answer is as far as what can we see and then what can we actually get to? The price of drugs on the street is the best indication that supply and demand—there is still a lot of stuff that is getting through. I think that is fair enough.

I think you said it yourself. Once we deploy technology, we all of a sudden see all the stuff that we didn't see before. It is not that they just started coming; it is just you can now see it. Is that a fair statement?

Mr. VITIELLO. I think it is fair as it relates to the state of the border reporting and when we are using the GEOINT and when we are using our own deployments.

Ms. MCSALLY. Yep.

Mr. VITIELLO. So it is accurate to say that the 56 percent number, that is a real-time deployment, so we know when it is happening in real time and can respond directly.

Ms. MCSALLY. Okay.

Mr. VITIELLO. In those other parts of the border, you may or may not need that kind of deployment, but, in the aggregate, you are aware of what is occurring over time.

Ms. MCSALLY. Okay.

So, going back to my original question, when the Arizona Technology Plan is complete—which I definitely want to make sure I understand when that is going to be complete, based on all the different parts of it—what level of, what you are kind-of calling situational awareness, but I guess what I am calling operational control—like, what will you be able to—real-time, you can see it moving across the border, what percentage of the, I think it is, you know, 360 miles of the Arizona border—it is the Arizona Technology Plan, so you are focusing on better technology for situational awareness in the Arizona border. What is the end goal? What is the end state?

Mr. VITIELLO. So that deployment is informed by agents on the ground that know how the technology works and know our own tactics for deployment and are aware of what the threat picture is. So, when those AORs are complete, we will have 100 percent monitoring of that border and being able to react in real time to all activity.

Now, there are limits to the technology. There are deep canyons. You have been to these places in Nogales where it is really difficult to see on the ground even with the technology.

Ms. MCSALLY. Right.

Mr. VITIELLO. But those deployments are designed for us to be 100 percent successful.

Ms. MCSALLY. Okay. So 100 percent is the goal.

So can you give me the time line of when all of the elements of the Arizona Technology Plan will be complete, as of right now?

I don't know if that is for you to answer or you, Mr. Borkowski.

Mr. VITIELLO. I think Mark is probably better——

Ms. MCSALLY. Okay.

Mr. VITIELLO [continuing]. To tell us the precise detail.

Mr. BORKOWSKI. The long and short of it is we believe Arizona will be done by fiscal year 2019.

Ms. MCSALLY. The end of fiscal year 2019?

Mr. BORKOWSKI. Yes.

Ms. MCSALLY. Okay.

Mr. BORKOWSKI. That is due to 2 specific areas of responsibility in the Tohono O'odham Nation. Except for those, the remote video surveillance system will be done by the end of this year; 3 out of the 5 AORs in Arizona for IFT will be done by the end of fiscal year 2017. Then it is those 2 areas of the Tohono O'odham Nation that lag in getting complete.

Ms. MCSALLY. Okay.

Just for expectations, too, for our constituents, in this fiscal year, what else is going in? I mean, the ranchers I was talking to last week——

Mr. BORKOWSKI. Right.

Ms. MCSALLY [continuing]. You know, the IFTs—can we just get a rundown of what is going in this fiscal year?

Mr. BORKOWSKI. Sure. So all of the remote video surveillance system, which are cameras and towers, the last area for that is Yuma. That is the last one to go in. That will be done by the end of this year.

For IFT, we are starting Douglas. Douglas should be complete toward the end of this year. Sonoita will start going contract this summer, so it should be done in about a year from that. So those are the key activities going on between now and, say, the summer of 2017.

Ms. MCSALLY. Okay.

So, fiscal year 2019, if everything is on track, the Arizona Technology Plan will be complete.

I know, Ms. Gambler, one of the points that you have pointed out is there has not been an integrated schedule. They have been sort of the piecemeal schedule. Is that still something you think is needed for the Arizona Technology Plan or for additional plans moving forward in Texas or other areas?

Ms. GAMBLER. Yeah, two points there, Chairwoman McSally.

No. 1, we still continue to believe that an integrated master schedule for the whole plan would help CBP better oversee the extent to which it is completing all of the programs under the plan within expected time frames. I know CBP disagrees with that. We continue to believe in that recommendation.

Second, as I mentioned earlier, for 2 of the programs under the plan, CBP has updated their schedules just for those programs. We will be looking at those 2 schedules going forward—we just recently received them—to see the extent to which they meet best practices, which has been some of our other recommendations. So, again, that is sort of an open question for us, but it is progress that they have updated the schedules.

Ms. MCSALLY. Great. Thank you.

I want to switch to a different topic, which is the use of tactical unmanned aerial systems or aerial vehicles. I know we talked about this in the first hearing I held.

I realize the Predator provides situational awareness sort-of at the operational or strategic level, but there are tools that are out there that we are currently using in the military where the agents could launch something that gives them situational awareness tactically.

I know you all mentioned that it is being looked into, but can I get a very specific answer as to whether there is a requirement and a move to provide tactical UAVs to our agents on the ground to improve situational awareness?

Mr. VITIELLO. So we do have an operational requirements document. So the Border Patrol at CBP, our partners in CBP writ large are convinced that this is a technology that needs to go into the hands of agents. We have made an operational requirements document, sort-of the official recognition of that. We are working with OTIA to understand what resources are available and how we would deploy them. We are in discussions with CBP Air and Marine to make sure that we are not in conflict as it relates to the airspace issues.

Then we have 2 projects, the same project underway with the Department of Homeland Security Science and Technology Directorate, in which they have helped us identify what resources are available, what the limitations for some of that resource is, so we can start to narrow on which platforms will be available to us.

We are in discussions for a memorandum of understanding with the FAA on the certificate of authorization. Again, that is part of the deconfliction piece. We are in a relationship with Naval Systems Command about contracting vehicles and about their own experience and best practices with using these elements.

We believe that we are very well on our way to start these deployments, because we think they are necessary for agents in the field.

Ms. MCSALLY. I agree.

Is one of the options—I don't know if there is any excess property from the DOD. Is one of the options excess property or just manufacturing capabilities that already are being deployed with the DOD as opposed to reinventing the wheel?

Mr. VITIELLO. So we are narrowing with S&T on what they call the RVSS program to decide which of the things are available either through DOD or through other vehicles for us to use.

Ms. MCSALLY. So what is the time line we are looking at for that?

Major General Alles, you can jump in.

Then, Ms. Gambler, I want to make sure there is a—you know, we don't want to have lessons identified that are actually lessons learned from past procurement buffoonery. So is this going along based on the lessons learned from previous procurement issues?

General Alles, do you want to pipe in?

Mr. ALLES. I was just going to mention one. We are going to do a near-term program with Border Patrol soon. But that is really to develop a COA in a particular area and apply the technology and see how it works before we move forward to any kind of procurement. So that would be step 1 in the process.

Just to note, the main problem here is the FAA still. So we can probably work out a COA and carve out a piece of airspace to work these smaller platforms in, but there are still no rules issued to actually operate these things, big picture, across the board. That still is coming and needs to be taken care of.

Ms. MCSALLY. Okay. Great.

Ms. Gambler.

Ms. GAMBLER. Yep, this is something that we are touching on as part of some of our on-going work, looking at, you know, this kind of small UAS program. So that is something we can certainly follow up with you on and try to give you some more information on going forward.

But it will be, you know, important for them to proceed, you know, in line with kind-of good acquisition management, you know, good testing, best practices, to ensure that, you know, to the extent that they do end up deploying some type of a system, that it meets requirements and that it is rolled out according to cost, schedule, and performance expectations.

Ms. MCSALLY. Great. Thank you.

I know I mentioned it last time, but Cochise College in southern Arizona is co-located there, and they have a great UAV program on the civilian side. They really want to have a conversation to partner on anything that might be rolled out, just to be able to, you know—not again having to reinvent training schools and operations that they already have on-going.

So I just want to lay that out there again, that I think these types of innovative partnerships like that would be really important if you are rolling anything like that forward.

I want to switch to ultralight detection. I think it was my first week in office, when I went back home, I got a full day with the Border Patrol team in the Tucson sector, to include a Black Hawk ride where a radar picked up a potential ultralight crossing, and we flew around in circles trying to find it. I was helping looking out the window, using my fighter pilot eyes, trying to help. It was like, you know, a needle in a haystack. It is impossible, as you know, very difficult to be able to detect these low-flying lightweight ultralights.

You know, the intended program to address that pretty much failed. So is there any additional technologies and programs we are looking at in order to solve this problem of the ultralight detection?

Mr. BORKOWSKI. Yes.

First of all, the ultralight threat when we started was high-urgency. So we went after this program that was not successful. If the ultralight threat were as urgent as it was, though, we would probably use those, because they actually could detect the ultralights; it is just they were very labor-intensive.

So we are looking for options to that. The urgency for the program is not as high as it was, but one of the things we are looking at is a DOD reuse system. There is a——

Ms. MCSALLY. Why is it not urgent anymore?

Mr. BORKOWSKI. We are seeing a tremendous decline in the number of ultralights.

Mr. ALLES. I will just mention the numbers. The high was in fiscal year 2010, 235. So far this year, 19.

Ms. MCSALLY. Do we know why that is?

Mr. ALLES. There are other methods of crossing the border to move the drugs, ma'am.

Ms. MCSALLY. Okay.

Mr. BORKOWSKI. So, again, I think if it jacked back up, we would probably go pull those ultralight aircraft detection systems and use them, because they would be worth it for that threat, but the threat has gone down.

Having said that, we have identified a couple of systems, one of which we have access to from DOD—it requires some modifications of software, and it is called a lightweight counter-mortar radar— that shows some potential here.

We also continue to do market research with industry. I don't always want to immediately go to DOD and, you know, foreclose opportunities for industry. There are other radars in industry as well.

But that is what we are looking at, and that lightweight counter-mortar radar looks very promising.

Ms. MCSALLY. Okay. Great. Thanks.

Do we know—I guess this would be to Mr. Borkowski.

Are there any other DOD excess property or any other technology that we know exists within the DOD that you all are looking at to get your hands on in order to help with the situational awareness?

Mr. BORKOWSKI. For situational awareness? Well, they obviously have kind-of common operating picture command-and-control-type systems that we look at. In fact, they have something called ART/TSOA, if you are familiar with that—Adaptive Red Team—where they bring a bunch of these industries in and plug them in. So we participate in those, and we look at those technologies.

With respect to, though, situational awareness, DHS S&T has what is called an Apex Program, because they are trying to get their arms around. As you can imagine, there is all kinds of stuff to sort through. So DHS S&T is doing a border situational awareness Apex Program basically to help us put all of that information together and to choose what is the right approach. I think that is where we will rely to make some smart decisions going forward.

Ms. MCSALLY. Okay. Great. Thank you.

Sorry. I am just firing off a bunch of questions here.

But I think it was in our first hearing I also asked a question about looking at putting VADER on manned aircraft. This is something that has been done in the past in other departments. Is there any looking into that, due to the limitations, both airspace and weather, of, you know, the Predator ops?

Mr. ALLES. So what we are looking at as an S&T effort is a lighter VADER-type system to put on our smaller aircraft, not necessarily the VADER operating on the UAS now. So that has been kind of the current direction we are looking at. We are looking at that, you know, through different, you know, technological venues.

So nothing substantial yet on that. We are really exploring the options at this point.

Ms. MCSALLY. Okay. Thanks.

Then, in between the tactical UAVs and the Predator, are there any other UAVs? There is a whole swath in that middle area there that are smaller and potentially cheaper. Is there any investigation or requirement that you are looking at to procure any, sort-of, mid-level UAVs? I just made up that terminology, but you know what I am saying—not quite the ones that the agents are deploying but not quite the Predator.

Mr. ALLES. So I think, to answer that, until we get full use out of the Predator in the airspace, I would actually not want to move in that direction. So, in my mind, the Predator actually fills the high and medium gap. What Chief Vitiello wants to do on the small side, which I think is a good effort, will fill the low-altitude gap.

But the real issue is I can get a Scan Eagle or something like that, I can't operate it in the airspace. The FAA won't let me.

Ms. MCSALLY. Yep.

Mr. ALLES. So the rules still prevent that. Until we can move beyond those and really get open use of the airspace with the Predator, that is going to be the limitation.

We are moving in that direction with the due-regard radar. We have a single Predator now equipped with that. We are going to test that and see if that is going to help open up the envelope with the FAA.

Ms. MCSALLY. Great. Thanks.

I want to move into the, kind-of, procurement process big picture. I know a lot of the things that Ms. Gambler, the GAO has pointed out, trying to move DHS more in line with practices in the DOD. Although I serve on the Armed Services Committee, and I will tell you, you know, there are good things about the DOD acquisition process, but that can also be quite painful and slow and bureaucratic and not nimble. By the time we get through all the machinations of the process, the technology has already changed, and, you know, we are late to the game.

So we are actually putting in, you know, the defense bill and additional legislation some changes to that process. So you don't necessarily want to mirror all of the DOD. You want to take the best of it but not the painful amounts of it. So, I mean, is that part of what is being looked at? Or are we just trying to mirror the DOD?

One of the issues in the DOD is getting project managers, contracting officers. It is basically human resources, human development, making sure we are recruiting, training, equipping, and keeping, retaining, you know, those that have this unique expertise that, thank God, I never had to have in the Air Force myself.

But on the manpower side and the development of expertise, I just wanted to hear perspectives on that and what is being done to address that issue.

Ms. GAMBLER. Sure.

So your first question first, on kind-of the DHS acquisition management process. I think the bottom line of GAO's reporting on this has been that, across the Department, not just with CBP but across the Department, DHS has a fairly sound, knowledge-based process for managing its acquisition. So that kind of foundational process, from our perspective, is in place.

Where DHS has fallen down has been on the execution. So what I mean by that is ensuring that acquisition programs go through that process, have approved acquisition documents before they move to the next phases in the process. That is where, kind-of, DHS has fallen down in terms of implementation. Again, they are making progress, but they still have a ways to go.

I might add that DHS acquisition management challenges are part of the reason why DHS management more broadly is part of GAO's high-risk list. So that is point No. 1.

The other point that I would make with regard to having the right acquisition management personnel in place to manage these programs, that also has been a challenge that GAO has reported on across the Department. It has also been something we have reported on related to CBP.

Some of the challenges that we identified in our last report regarding why some of the programs under the Arizona Technology Plan were not meeting schedule had to do with CBP and OITA not always having the resources in place they needed to manage the acquisitions, review some of the proposals, and that kind of thing.

So that, I think, has been a challenge in the past for DHS and for CBP.

Ms. McSally. Mr. Borkowski, do you want to add anything to that?

Mr. Borkowski. Yes, I think that is exactly right.

Now, certainly, obviously, DHS is working on this. So, for example, I understand this issue about documentation, but I will tell you that Under Secretary Deyo and Deputy Under Secretary Fulghum have, frankly, been beating the, you know, stuffing out of us. A lot of emphasis on getting that document current. We had a big push at the end of last year. Mr. Fulghum made a commitment to the Congress, and we all got that word, and we did that. So that is clearly an area of emphasis.

This area of expertise in program management is a big threat issue. We have spent a great deal of time on it. We have a Homeland Security Acquisition Institute; we have sent people to school. But the experience is the big thing.

A lot of my time is occupied on running reviews of programs, not so much to collect status but to start getting people to understand what it means to review a program. What does cost even mean? You know, for example, cost in acquisition really means, did you get for a dollar what you expected to get? But you will get a lot of conversation about, do I have the budget? That is a different question. So understanding what a baseline is, the basics of program management.

I will tell you I think we have made tremendous progress over the last few years. But you can imagine what that does to acquisition, when you are doing the training while you are deploying. Those have been challenges.

Then, of course, getting enough people and not burning people out, as we discussed with Mr. Thompson, is another issue.

Ms. McSally. Are you actively recruiting from the DOD those that are separating or retiring?

Mr. Borkowski. In terms of acquisition positions, we don't actually go to DOD and ask for people. However, we get a lot of DOD applicants to our open applications. So I think the word gets out.

Ms. McSally. It seems like that is where the experience would be, right?

Mr. Borkowski. Yes.

Ms. McSally. So, I mean—although maybe they are leaving and they want to go do something else. But, certainly, if they have the experience in program management, that would be, you know, transferable skills.

Mr. Borkowski. Right.

Ms. McSally. Okay.

I am going to keep going here. I have a couple more.

Chief Vitiello, I don't know if it is for you or General Alles or both. Can you let us know when the CGAP analysis is going to be available or to be shared with us here in Congress?

Mr. Vitiello. So we are happy to work with you on a schedule to catch you up to where we think we are. But CGAP, by its design and the work that we did with applied physics at Johns Hopkins, is an iterative process.

Ms. McSally. Okay.

Mr. Vitiello. So what we have done up until now is sort-of learn the process and learn the best practices, which comes from our own experience plus what they have learned, along with DOD, to help us identify what the mission needs are, how to fill capability gaps, and what the use case is for identified technologies or changes in tactics, et cetera.

So what we have done is we have trained a majority of the workforce that are deployed in an effort to understand the process, what CGAP is, how to apply it in their own AOR, and then feed us that information at the headquarters to then turn in to requirements. Then we can push over with our requirements folks in our office and then over to OTIA to move the process forward.

So we would be happy to come back and give you sort-of a detailed brief about the number of people that have been trained, the kinds of discoveries that we have made, and asking agents for their feedback, how they would solve particular problems; look at the material resources, like we need a tower, we need a sensor, we need a tripwire, and then the other, the non-material things, like consequences and things that happen maybe post-arrest or information exchange with other departments, et cetera.

So we would be happy to come back and give you sort-of the full range of what has been trained and what it is designed to do and then what the roll-up report looks like, but recognizing that it is iterative. As the threats change, as conditions change——

Ms. McSally. Right.

Mr. Vitiello [continuing]. We want to be able to update those plans so that we are not investing in last year's problem but are working ahead.

Ms. McSally. Great.

General Alles.

Mr. Alles. I think on the Air and Marine side we are in the early stages of it. We would expect our really first substantial output to be about a year away. So they are currently early in the process, as discussed. As the chief mentioned, it is an iterative process, but we would expect a more substantial output here really next summer.

Ms. McSally. Okay. Great. Thank you. Yeah, let's follow up. I don't know if some of it is Classified, but maybe with a briefing we could do later on, just to kind-of see where we are at.

You mentioned it, Chief Vitiello, but the actual agents are part of that process, right? It is not just the sector leadership and above?

Mr. Vitiello. That is correct. So the people who are involved in the planning for their particular area.

Ms. MCSALLY. Yeah.

Mr. VITIELLO. So the station level, the people who are actually deploying on the ground, are taking feedback from the people who are making the arrests, who are deploying and they are looking at the line each and every day. That feeds up into the station, rolled up to the sector each, and then that comes back to us. People are trained in each of those processes to then feed to us. Then that turns into requirements, it turns into forecasts for budgets and programming, et cetera.

Ms. MCSALLY. Great. Thanks.

General Alles, I want to follow up on my earlier question on getting information to the agents. I know the Big Pipe allows the Predator feed to get to a desktop, but is there something in the works to actually get it to an iPad or something that is more mobile for the agents?

Mr. ALLES. Yes, ma'am. A couple things there.

So, first off, we are pursuing the Minotaur system. This is a Naval Air Systems Command system that is used on their patrol aircraft to distribute information. So that is essential for us to take information off our platforms—radar information, the EOIR, signals information—and actually put it into a system that can redistribute it to other assets that have Minotaur. It goes back to the AMOC in Riverside and can be sent back out.

In terms of local agents, part of that is what Chief mentioned in terms of looking down the Blue Force Tracker route. We can already send video. We can distribute what is called a carry viewer to agents on the ground so they can actually see video if that is desired. Typically, we are using, you know, actually, radio information to cue the agents.

There is a system we are looking at, which the name eludes me, which will allow us to put that information on something like an Android phone or an iPhone, which can actually form its own local network, which could be advantageous for us in terms of sending video from aircraft down to actual agents on the ground.

So those are the directions we are going. I would say there is a lot of work to be done there.

I think on the, kind-of, investigation side, supporting his or those, we are able to move the video very easily in those areas and give it to agents on the ground. In the more remote areas, that is still an area that we need substantial work in.

Ms. MCSALLY. Great. Thanks.

I also want to ask you, General Alles, about—the National Guard has been supplementing with, you know, some of the air assets, but this last year my understanding is that their number of hours or support was cut in half.

When you guys are doing the CGAP analysis, are there assumptions made on National Guard capabilities that are a part of your plan, or are they assumed to not be there? How is that impacting your operations or the gaps?

Mr. ALLES. So, I mean, from our standpoint, a couple things. First off, in the areas where we were using the National Guard hours, we have made a substantial move of our assets into those locations. So, in the south Texas area in particular, we have increased our assets by over 50 percent, along with our flight hours have gone up proportionally also.

In actually doing the CGAP analysis, we are not necessarily counting on their support. As you are aware from the Armed Services side, they have had substantial cuts in the DOD budget. I mean, I have been reading the articles on the Marine Corps and getting 30- or 40-percent readiness rates on their aircraft. So they have major challenges there.

So we aren't necessarily looking for that in the analysis. We are looking to support the Border Patrol and our other operations with our own internal assets and analyze the gaps in that method.

Ms. McSALLY. Okay. Great. Thanks.

Mr. Borkowski, can you talk about how you are sharing requirements with industry so they can spend their R&D dollars to meet, you know, agents' needs? Or how do you engage with industry earlier in the process, you know, searching for new technology?

Mr. BORKOWSKI. Well, we do that through a whole bunch of ways. So, first of all, when I am in town, I have probably a meeting a day with anybody who wants to come and talk to me. Sometimes they want to tell me what they have got; sometimes they want us to discuss generally our issues.

We have reverse industry days, where we talk to industry about our requirements. We speak at any number of conferences, where we list our technology interests for industry. We also work very closely with DHS S&T that has a very extensive outreach program, including to nontraditional industry, right? Because it is kind of easy to get to the traditional people because they know how to connect with us, but the nontraditionals.

Ms. McSALLY. Right.

Mr. BORKOWSKI. So we have a whole bunch of ways that we talk to them.

Now, the tricky thing is when we are getting ready for an acquisition. That is where we have a more focused discussion about: What are the requirements, how should we depict them, what would industry be able to respond to. Then things get a lot more detailed.

But in advance of that, it is a more general discussion of, these are our interests in technology areas, this is what we think we plan to do over the next few years. We do that through a number of mechanisms.

Ms. McSALLY. Great. Thanks.

All right. I am about to wrap up, but I want to give the opportunity for all the witnesses, if there is anything else that you didn't get to share in your opening statement or through the questions that came out. Is there anything else that any of you want to present on the record for the committee?

Chief.

Mr. VITIELLO. Well, thank you for this opportunity. Just to reiterate some of the testimony and what is in the prepared remarks, we are interested in having the most effective and efficient sustainable technology that is available.

I think it is important—and I think we have heard this today—that we will never be as fast as the market to bring these things into the hands of agents. We have wonderful men and women out there that have really great ideas about how to do the job more efficiently, but the bureaucracy doesn't always support that rapid acquisition and putting those things in their hands as quickly as even we would like them to.

But they are our best assets as it relates to that last—what we call the last 50 meters. You have to have people on the ground that support the technology, that the technology has to support them. But, at the end of the day, they are the ones that have to make contact with whatever that threat is.

So we appreciate them for that work. We appreciate you, in your oversight role, in helping us prepare them to give us the tools that they deserve to be successful. So thanks for that.

Ms. MCSALLY. Great. Thanks, Chief.

General Alles.

Mr. ALLES. I would just like to thank the committee generally for the, you know, support they give to the agency in terms of us performing our mission. You know, not only the oversight part of it, but also the interest of the committee Members—multiple trips and, you know, looking at the stuff that we are working on.

I could list a list of things that we want. We can provide that off-line. But just appreciate the participation of the committee.

Ms. MCSALLY. Absolutely. Thanks, General Alles.

Mr. Borkowski.

Mr. BORKOWSKI. I would just add that, recognizing the committee's frustration, we certainly have appreciated the continued support despite the frustration. It has been very significant to us, and it has helped us a great deal.

As we do go forward, I would like to have continued discussion about what do we do about the cultural and structural impediments, because the biggest beating I get is on time. Yes, cost and performance are important. I think we have done okay there. But the time is killing us all.

Some of that, I think, will require a different thinking about how we accept risk. Because to innovate takes risk, and that means occasionally we will have failures. What is the right risk tolerance? Frankly, the community that works in this business is very risk-averse, and that is one of the things we really have to crack.

But I appreciate the opportunity to testify, and I appreciate the committee's continued support.

Ms. MCSALLY. Absolutely. Those are the same types of discussions we are having, by the way, on the Armed Services Committee related to the DOD.

Ms. Gambler.

Ms. GAMBLER. I just want to say thank you for inviting us to testify today.

Just some of the last items that we were talking about here, in terms of ultralight detection, the CGAP process, technology metrics, we do have on-going work for the subcommittee in a number of those areas. So we would be happy to follow up with you and your staff to brief you at any time, and look forward to that work coming out in the future here as well.

Ms. MCSALLY. Great. Thanks, Ms. Gambler. I appreciate it.

All right. I want to thank all the witnesses for your valuable testimony and the Members for their questions.

The Members may have some additional questions for the witnesses. We will ask you to respond to these, please, in writing. Pursuant to committee rule 7(e), the hearing record will be held open for 10 days.

Without objection, the committee stands adjourned.

[Whereupon, at 4:21 p.m., the subcommittee was adjourned.]

○

www.ingramcontent.com/pod-product-compliance
Lightning Source LLC
Chambersburg PA
CBHW081126180526
45170CB00008B/3024